Hidden Ontario

HIDDEN ONTARIO
Secrets from Ontario's Past

~ SECOND EDITION ~

TERRY BOYLE

DUNDURN
TORONTO

Editor: Matt Baker
Design: Courtney Horner
Printer: Webcom

Library and Archives Canada Cataloguing in Publication

Boyle, Terry
        Hidden Ontario : secrets from Ontario's past / Terry Boyle.

Includes bibliographical references and index.
Issued also in electronic formats.
ISBN 978-1-55488-955-6

        1. Ontario--History, Local. I. Title.

FC3061.B685 2011   971.3   C2011-901175-1

1   2   3   4   5   15   14   13   12   11

 Conseil des Arts du Canada   Canada Council for the Arts    Canadä   ONTARIO ARTS COUNCIL / CONSEIL DES ARTS DE L'ONTARIO

We acknowledge the support of the **Canada Council for the Arts** and the **Ontario Arts Council** for our publishing program. We also acknowledge the financial support of the **Government of Canada** through the **Canada Book Fund** and **Livres Canada Books,** and the **Government of Ontario** through the **Ontario Book Publishing Tax Credit,** and the **Ontario Media Development Corporation.**

Care has been taken to trace the ownership of copyright material used in this book. The author and the publisher welcome any information enabling them to rectify any references or credits in subsequent editions.

J. Kirk Howard, President

Printed and bound in Canada.
www.dundurn.com

Dundurn 3 Church Street, Suite 500 Toronto, Ontario, Canada M5E 1M2	Gazelle Book Services Limited White Cross Mills High Town, Lancaster, England LA1 4XS	Dundurn 2250 Military Road Tonawanda, NY U.S.A. 14150

MIX
Paper from
responsible sources
FSC www.fsc.org   FSC® C004071

Contents

Introduction

History is always relevant. To understand our present and to plan for our future we need, somehow, to relate to our past. We can't look at everything — it just isn't possible, but perhaps we can find some doors previously unlocked, some tales almost forgotten. We can look at some chronology that creates a pathway back to the present; we can examine occurrences that remind us that the flow of time was meant to bring growth and change, evolution. This book is an opportunity for all of those things.

A book should be an inspiration. A history book should be an invitation to review, to explore, to reminisce, to discover, to travel, to unravel. I want to take you to the past in your mind and inspire you to visit it in the present. Visit museums. Listen to our elders. Discover the stories behind the places. Learn to question when you travel, to open your awareness to all that was, is, will be, could be.

History is alive. You can see it. Sometimes you can taste it. Often you can feel it. I love it. Let me share it with you.

Acton

It hits you when you walk through the doors: the massive space, the quiet, the rich earth-colours, the soft and strong textures, and a certain pungent smell that only comes from one thing. Here is Canada's largest store of its kind and one that gives the whole town a nickname — Leathertown! This is Acton, and we are in The Olde Hide House.

The story of Acton and its leather industry began in 1829 when Rufus Adams and his two brothers, Zenas and Ezra, arrived in the area and purchased land to farm. Ezra built a gristmill on his property. The Adams brothers opted to survey their farms into town lots and called the settlement "Adamsville." In 1833 Rufus Adams purchased the land where the The Olde Hide House is situated today. By 1842 Abraham Nelles established the first tannery in Adamsville. The Adams brothers' combined holdings, at that time, had reached approximately 500 acres. In 1844 the postmaster, Robert Swan, renamed the village "Acton" in honour of his birthplace in Northumberland, England.

The ownership of the various parcels into which Rufus Adams's original lot had been divided changed hands several times over the ensuing years. In 1856 the Grand Trunk Railway ran a rail line through it and opened the Acton Train Station.

The tannery industry was flourishing, and in 1852 Abraham Nelles's tannery was sold to Messrs. Coleman and McIntryre of Dundas, Ontario. It burned down that very same year and was rebuilt. It was, in turn, acquired by the firm of McCloshen and Atcheson, who turned it over to Sessins, Toby and Co.; George L. Beardmore purchased it in 1865.

Thus a period of frequent turnover ended, as the tannery stayed in the Beardmore family for more than half a century.

The Beardmore family had been associated with tanning in Ontario since 1840. George Beardmore was born in Islington, London, England, on February 16, 1818. At the age of 14 he sailed from Bristol to Canada. He returned to England in November 1838 in a bit of a quandary. He was a very religious young man and had considerable trouble reconciling his burning desire for wealth with his pastoral beliefs. April 1839 was a turning point, and he and his younger brother, Joseph, left for Canada.

In 1840 the two brothers built the first stone tannery building in Canada, in Hamilton. The foundation for the building was laid on March 31, 1840. The Beardmores worked hard and improved, expanded and created a successful leather business. On the night of July 11, 1840, disaster struck. The tannery was destroyed by fire.

Joseph Beardmore's health failed and he returned to England on April 15, 1846. He died at the age of 33 in 1852. Two years later George re-established himself in Toronto, where he engaged in business as a leather merchant and at the same time continued to supply the trade in Hamilton. He then bought a small tannery at Grand River which was later destroyed by fire. Next, he bought a tannery in Guelph. In 1865 he closed shop in Guelph and headed to Acton, where he purchased the Sessions, Toby and Co. tannery in 1865.

George Beardmore's four sons all followed him into the business and became partners. They were Walter D. Beardmore, 1849–1915; George W. Beardmore, 1851–1934; Alfred Beardmore, 1859–1946; and Fred Beardmore, 1871–1967.

The role a tannery played was extremely important to the economics of a settlement. The tannery was a great help to homesteaders who were clearing their land. The settlers felled hemlock trees, peeled their bark, and piled and delivered them to the tannery for cash during the winter months. The *Acton Free Press* once reported farmers bringing bark to the tannery at a rate of 20 to 30 loads at a time, by teams, in a long string, down the main street of Acton.

The hemlock spruce were not considered to have any other value before the Second World War, and whole stands of these trees were clear-cut just for the bark, the wood left in the bush to rot. The bark, on average, contained 8–10 percent tannin. This tannin solution produced a firm, quality leather with a reddish cast.

In 1872 a serious fire at the Acton tannery destroyed most of the buildings, but the Beardmores rebuilt immediately. By 1876 hemlock bark was in critical supply and the Beardmores decided to move their tanning operations to Bracebridge in the Muskokas. Mr. Charles Knees, a native of Sweden, took over the Acton tannery in 1877 and tanned horsehide for shoe uppers.

By 1887 the Beardmores, while maintaining operations in Muskoka, returned to Acton, repurchased the tannery, and began the tanning of belt leather. The Beardmores' holdings were considerable by now and new buildings were erected. Eventually, the main Beardmore tanneries in Acton had a combined floor space of nearly 100,000 square metres (1,000,000 square feet), one of the largest tanning operations in the British Empire.

In 1889 Beardmore and Company built a large brick warehouse (the present site of the Olde Hide House) next to the railway line. When the raw hides were brought in by rail, they were stored here and then transported by horse-drawn wagons to the tannery for processing. Finished leather was also stored in this building, while awaiting transportation by rail to other destinations. This arrangement soon proved to be unsatisfactory, as the route from the warehouse to the plant passed through a low-lying, swampy area that proved to be almost impassable in the spring months. The problem was solved when a spur line was built from the main rail line to the Beardmore plant, making direct shipments possible.

In 1933 the warehouse was no longer required and was sold to Amos Mason for $1,500. Mr. Mason established the Mason Knitting Company in the building and continued operation until 1969. That year the property was sold to Frank Heller and Company, a firm that specialized in the production of split leather.

In June 1980 Fred Dawkins, Ron Heller, and Don Dawkins purchased the building and The Olde Hide House Company in an effort to re-establish Acton's leather heritage. Both families had several generations of experience in various aspects of the leather industry. Don Dawkins, the president and general manager of the Olde Hide House, his wife Faye, and sons Stephen, David, and Jamie, acquired the controlling interest in the firm in 1982.

The nature and scope of the activities conducted in the acre-sized building have varied over the years. At one point, one-third of the building was devoted to arts and crafts studios (including glass-blowing and pottery); from 1983 until 1994 a restaurant called Jack Tanner's Table occupied almost 20 percent of the building. Today, the entire 3,000-square-metre (32,000 square feet) structure is devoted to the merchandising of leather garments, furniture, accessories, and gifts, making The Olde Hide House not only the largest leather goods store in Canada, but the largest anywhere in the world. In 1999 nearly 250,000 visitors came from more than 43 countries, and they signed the leather-bound guest book in the store's front foyer. Any trip to Acton should include the sensory experience of The Olde Hide House.

Often a main industry will dominate the profile of a town, but if you like a little mystery, Acton has some of that, too. Most visitors are completely unaware that the town hall is haunted.

The building was constructed in 1882, to house the municipal council, at a cost of $4,574. An expansive public hall and stage on the second floor, with dancing and other entertainments, served as a social centre for the village. The main floor of the building accommodated the village constable and a lock-up cell for prisoners — it's still in place today. During the onset of regional government in 1974, the town hall was slated for demolition, but a group of concerned citizens saved the historic building. In 1983 Heritage Acton purchased the town hall for $1.00 and began renovations. They did not, however, manage to renovate or relocate the ghost!

Some people believe Jimmy, the former caretaker of the building, is the ghost. Jimmy was a very quiet, hermit-like individual who shied away from people. Sometime after his death, in 1946, footsteps and sweeping sounds would be heard on the upper floor of the town hall.

The architect hired to work on the restoration project in the 1980s actually managed to photograph the shadowy outline of a human form on the empty second floor. On another occasion a reporter, touring the building, was taken upstairs and suddenly felt a cold shiver down one side of her body. She thought a window had been left open, but soon discovered that the windows hadn't been opened in years.

In the fall of 1997, a reporter from Acton's Halton Cable Network slept overnight in an attempt to capture Jimmy on film. Although he felt nothing unusual, he left his camera turned on, just in case. The next day when the film was developed, he discovered a fleeting image of a floating light in the shape of a face. The shape was suspended in space. Jimmy was well-known for not wishing to be disturbed at night.

Whether you like a sensory experience or an extra-sensory experience, Acton will give you both, so be sure to add it to your itinerary.

Algonquin Provincial Park

Algonquin Provincial Park stretches across 7,725 square kilometres of wild and majestic lakes and forests, bogs and rivers, cliffs and beaches, making it the canoeists' and campers' paradise of Ontario. Algonquin is Ontario's best-known recreation camping facility — but it has a history that's sometimes less than pretty.

Small groups of Natives dotted this corner of the province where they fished, hunted, and savoured the berries that grew plentifully here. Algonquin was the generic name given to these Natives by the French. The name was once thought to have derived from *Algomequin*, meaning "those on the other side," but a newer theory is that the word comes from the Micmac *Algoomaking*, meaning "at the place of spearing fish."

It wasn't long before the Natives had company. First it was the fur trappers, who discovered the area and moved in to take advantage of the abundant wildlife. Next, in the early 1800s, army surveyors arrived, among them Lieutenant Baddeley of the Royal Engineers. He was following orders to survey a route to link the "old colonies" in Upper Canada with the "western outposts" of the province, since most of the colonization roads ended there. At about the same time, two pioneer families, Dennison and Dufond, also settled in the district.

Industrious loggers pushed their way up from the Ottawa River in search of the great white pine trees, the primary wood in demand in Britain. Their need for wood could not be satisfied until the last pine was felled, and the loggers' path was easily followed, as it was a trail of devastation. The lumber gangs lived in remote, primitive camps

Archives of Ontario

Tom Thomson in Algonquin Park. Always a struggle to paint or fish! He was known to lose painting supplies when passion rocked his boat.

throughout the area and felled and squared the giant pine. When the spring came they drove them down swollen tributaries into the Ottawa River and on to the rest of the world.

The lumber companies were many in the 1850s — McLachin, J.D. Shier, J.R. Booth, Barnet and Gilmour, and many more. The government felt that once the timber had been cleared, the land would be suitable for homesteading. The settlers disagreed. They found the soil sandy and shallow and had to turn to trapping or working for the lumber companies in order to survive.

By the latter half of the 19th century, the Algonquin area was in a state of utter devastation. Lumbering had increased so rapidly and over such vast expanses that the people of Ontario were greatly concerned about the future of the forests, the water, and the wildlife. Concern was also voiced about the waterways, because the Algonquin region was the headwater for five major rivers: the Petawawa, Bonnechere, Madawaska, Oxtongue, and Amable.

It took vision and government support to resolve the situation. Alexander Kirkwood had the vision. Mr. Kirkwood was born in Belfast, Ireland, in 1822 and lived there until 1846. He left for America that year and farmed there until coming to Montreal in 1853, where he again he took up farming. While working with Robert Nugent Watts at Rivière St. Francis, he wrote an article for the *Montreal Agriculturist* entitled "Drilling of Wheat." Malcolm Cameron, minister of the Department of Agriculture, read the article and sent for Mr. Kirkwood. In a matter of days, he was dispatched to Europe to report on "the growth and management of flax on the Continent of Europe." Upon his return he was given an appointment in the Crown Lands Department and remained there until his retirement.

During those years he was a tireless worker. He wrote for many publications and became interested in Canadian fisheries. He and J.G. Murphy, of the Cree Grants and Sales Department, published a joint work on the "undeveloped lands of northern Ontario." This work attracted interest and praise. Mr. Kirkwood ultimately introduced systematic forestry into Canada. It was through his foresight that the Algonquin Forest and Park was set aside for natural use and enjoyment. (Thank you, Alexander Kirkwood).

In 1885 he began to advocate controls on trapping and on the cutting of timber in the area. He wrote to the land commissioner of Ontario, the Honourable T.B. Pardee, to suggest that they create a park and name it Algonquin National Park, in honour of the Natives who once occupied the region. Nonetheless, it was not until 1892 that a Royal Commission was set up to study the feasibility of Kirkwood's idea. Finally, in 1893, an act of Parliament was passed that designated the region a conservation area "for the use and enjoyment of the people." In lieu of "national" they chose "provincial," and Algonquin Provincial Park was born.

Did this mean that the lumbering operations were stopped forever? No! The act did not entirely stop logging operations in the park. Not long after the act was passed, construction began on the Ottawa, Arnprior and Parry Sound Railway, which was completed in 1897. Rail transportation was important to the logging industry, and logging companies now saw fit to strip portions of forest in the southwestern section of the park. These lumber companies even built spur lines that could be dismantled once the best trees were cut. It wasn't until 1959, 65 years after the birth of the park, that rail service was discontinued.

The first white woman known to visit the Algonquin region was Susanna Moodie, a noted Canadian writer. She and her family took a canoe trip into the area in 1835. Other artists were also drawn to Algonquin and some never left. It was the rugged wilderness and incredible terrain that drew them. The first group, a small party of painters, arrived on Canoe Lake in 1902: W.W. Alexander, David Thomson, and Robert Holmes. They were eager to visit some of the remaining lumber camps and explored Opeongo, the largest lake in the park. They were followed by other artists such as J.W. Beatty, J.E.H. McDonald, Arthur Lismer, A.Y. Jackson, and a young man by the name of Tom Thomson.

Algonquin Park meant many things to this talented artist. Each summer Thomson explored the wilderness, and, inspired by what he saw, captured the essence of Canada in his celebrated paintings. In 1917, a tragedy took place: Tom Thomson died! Some say he drowned, accidentally, in Canoe Lake, while others whispered murder. Whatever happened, it remains both a mystery and a great loss of artistic talent.

Highway 60, running through the southwestern corner of the park, was completed in 1935, and from 1947 to 1948 it was paved. In 1972 more than 60,000 visitors camped in the park's interior. Three years later 683,661 tourists enjoyed the park — 10 times as many!

To celebrate the 100th anniversary of Algonquin Park, a visitor centre was opened in 1993. The centre has world-class exhibits on the natural and human history of the park, a relaxing restaurant, an excellent bookstore, and "The Algonquin Room," which holds exhibitions of Algonquin art, then and now. A theatre presentation sums up the park story, and a viewing deck puts in all in perspective.

Visitors interested in the logging history of the park can visit the Algonquin Logging Museum, located just inside the east gate. The museum brings the story of logging to life, from the early square timber days to the last of the great river drives.

Algonquin Park also offers the canoeist 1,500 kilometres (about 930 miles) of canoe routes throughout the district. The backpacker has a choice of three trails to hike: the Highland, Western Uplands, or Eastern Pines. These trails have loops ranging from 6 to 88 kilometres (4 to 55 miles) in length.

Although the Park is, to some, overburdened with campers, the wilderness camper still has a few choices, but they have to work harder, go farther, and settle for more company along the way. It is an excellent place to holiday, a great learning experience for children, and it remains an inspirational landscape for painters and photographers alike. Let us give a salute to the foresight of Alexander Kirkwood, and others who followed, for correcting the path of less-than-pretty history!

Bala

For more than half a century, dancers and music lovers have frolicked beneath the moon and stars to the chords that drifted and echoed from Dunn's Pavillion. For more than a century, tourists, fishermen, and hunters have thronged by horse and buggy, by train, by boat, and by automobile to this picturesque setting that winds around Lake Muskoka and the wide Moon River. Magnificent hotels, quaint stone churches, humble and glorious summer houses — they are all here in one of Ontario's tiniest towns, the Cranberry Capital of Ontario, Bala.

From the beginning, Thomas Burgess endeavoured to ensure that food and shelter, the two essentials of life, were available in the settlement. He opened a general store, a bake shop, a blacksmith shop, and operated a supply boat. As a responsible and concerned citizen, Burgess devoted his time to local matters. He was instrumental in the settlement of a group of Mohawks, a First Nations band from Oka, Quebec, from 1868 into the 1870s. Chief Louis Sahanatien needed help to transport his people and their goods across the 19 kilometres (12 miles) of trackless forest to the shores of Black Lake in Gibson Township. For many years Burgess voluntarily acted as agent between the Natives and the Department of Indian Affairs. In 1892 he donated land for a church in the community of Bala.

More settlers followed Burgess, and they worked hard to establish their settlement. Mr. and Mrs. Henry C. Guy opened a boarding house which later became the Bala Falls Hotel. Mrs. Guy was also responsible for establishing the first educational facility in Bala by teaching in her own home. The families of Ephraim B. Sutton, George Clements, Alfred Jackson, John Board, Thomas Currie, John May, Joseph Spencer, Richard Moore, William Carr, Henry Hurling, and the Hamills were also among Bala's earliest pioneers.

Bala, at one time, was known as Musquosh Falls. A post office was established here under the name of Muskoka in 1870, but the community was eventually named Bala. Thomas Burgess had, at one time, lived in the Bala Lake district of Wales and, having been impressed by the natural beauty there, he named his community correspondingly.

Rose and Ephraim (fondly known as E.B.) Sutton emigrated from England in 1882 and, on the advice of Mr. A.P. Cockburn and Thomas Burgess, settled in the district and eventually built the Swastika Hotel (now called the Bala Bay Hotel).

The Sutton family moved to the community of Bala in 1899 and opened a general store. In December 1901, E.B. Sutton established contracts for the first telephone line to connect with one operated by the Great North Western Telegraph Company from Bracebridge to Port Sandfield. Sutton also worked as a correspondent to Bracebridge, Gravenhurst, and Orillia weekly newspapers. He was adamant about environmental issues and especially protested against farmers who built barns on slopes that went down to the water, and warned tourists not to use the lakes for bathing.

Fred Sutton, his son, shared some of his memories: "Many were the hardships of which my parents told me. Dad spent much of his time working for Mr. Burgess at Bala. Pioneering was hard on men but harder still on women left so much alone in the bush. Early reading had filled their minds with dread of wild animals and even wilder 'savage' Indians. I can just imagine my Mother's perturbation when, while all alone, a Native called and asked to see the Boss. Mother, of course, said he would soon be in; the man seated himself just inside and said he would wait. Hours later, when Dad returned, it transpired the Indian wanted to borrow a gun. What a quandary! Not wishing to make a bad start by offending a Native, the gun was lent and the folks went to bed thinking they had seen the last of their gun. Morning came, and, lo and behold, the gun and a hindquarter of venison were hanging in the porch."

Archives of Ontario

Bala Railway Station in August of 1916. A sultry summer eve sees a group in their whites relax while waiting for trip back to Hogtown. As better highways were built to service cottage country north of Toronto, weekend passenger service by both the CPR and CNR was phased out after the Second World War. This particular station was dismantled in the 1970s.

In 1910 E.B. and Fred built the first three-storey brick hotel in Bala. They named their establishment the Swastika Hotel after the ancient swastika symbol — a symbol for well-being and benediction in the form of a Greek cross with each arm bent at a right angle. The Suttons had purchased the property from Thomas Burgess, who sold it to them on the condition that alcohol would never be sold on the property. They had agreed. Hotel guests were able to stroll the 23-acre site, go horseback riding on the trails located behind the building, go boating, and indulge in the fabulous meals and warm hospitality.

It wasn't long before the district of Bala supported a number of small farms with cattle and sheep. Bala also had the unique distinction of becoming incorporated as a town in 1914, without ever having had the status of a village. The first mayor was one of Thomas Burgess's sons, Dr. A.M. Burgess.

Fred Sutton once shared this about Bala: "Tourists and sportsmen had discovered the beauties of this area and created a demand for

Courtesy of Bob Sutton

Tourists enjoy a horseback ride at the Swastika Hotel in Bala. This three-storey brick hotel was built in 1910 by E.B. Sutton and his son Fred. The hotel name changed during the Second World War. Today, we know it as the Bala Bay Hotel.

accommodation. Hotels and boarding houses sprang into being. Muskoka lamb supplied to the resort hotels became so famous for its special appeal to the palate that posh hotels and restaurants in New York City made a feature of Muskoka Lamb on their menus."

Fred also recalled an eccentric character who came to the Swastika Hotel: "In August, 1926, a guest arrived in a Ford Coupe and registered as Captain Venus. He was wearing a Mountie's hat and claimed to be a member of the Force. He explained the absence of his tunic by saying it was at the cleaners. His personality was likable and conversation interesting. We seated him at my own table and we enjoyed his company.

"During the day he policed the area, controlling traffic, ordering defective cars off the road, and so on. An elderly lady, with her nurse/companion, happened to be staying at the hotel at the same time. The nurse, probably suffering from boredom and thinking we were having too much fun with the Mountie, persuaded me to move him to their table. He very gallantly squired the lady on canoe trips and walks and, incidentally, borrowed 10 dollars. Late the second day, I was surprised to see two uniformed Mounties at the desk asking for Captain Venus. They were sent to his room and they all went out together a few minutes later. I was on the point of retiring when Venus came in and asked for his bill. Next morning I found he had spent the night in the lock-up.

"We discovered later that he was a mental patient from Whitby, Ontario. Shell-shocked in World War I, he had a fine war record, in fact, among some papers found in his room was a letter from a commanding officer recommending him for the Victoria Cross. His mental quirks caused him to run away from the institution and pose as a person of authority.

"The *Toronto Star* of September 25th, 1926, reported at some length the story I have just told and another escapade of his at Port Hope, Ontario. There he apparently posed as an officer from the Department of Health; he closed dairies and generally caused havoc with the local Board of Health.

"I rather suspect it was the nurse's ten-spot that paid my bill."

Today it is said the Bala Bay Inn is haunted. It may be the ghost of Thomas Burgess, upset that alcohol is now served in his establishment — or it may be E.B., who promised to communicate from "the other side."

Bala, with numerous shops and parks along the river and bay side, is still a major tourist centre during the summer months. Among the shops there is a very special art gallery, right on the main street of Bala. The owner and operator is Carol News, a member of Wahta First Nations Mohawk community. High quality carvings, paintings, beading, basketry, and some other materials can be had in the gallery.

Each year a major cranberry festival occurs the weekend after Thanksgiving. Local cranberry growers, the Johnsons, offer guided tours of their operation and sell a variety of cranberry products, including their very own cranberry wine. It is truly a learning experience, not to mention a lot of fun, to explore their cranberry marsh. Artisans also arrive that weekend to set up along the main streets and in the arena; here we are, now in the 21st century, and Dunn's Pavillion is still humming and freshly painted.

The Baldoon Mysteries

Fact or fiction, what you are about to read supposedly took place more than 160 years ago and remains an incredible tale in the history of Ontario.

Our story begins with John McDonald and his family, who experienced several spine-tingling events in a place called Baldoon. Nervous of future occurrences and the possibility that their lives were in danger, the McDonalds struggled against invisible dark forces. They were plagued by some malevolent energy that interrupted their lives and defied explanation. Nothing seemed to function as it should. Surely, they had been cursed.

What was Baldoon really like? The community was located in southwestern Ontario on low, wet lands that were surveyed in 1802. It was Lord Alexander Selkirk who sought to attract Scottish Highlanders to the area. In return for this, Selkirk himself would be granted 150 acres for every colonist he procured. It would seem that the settlement of Baldoon was founded on less-than-benevolent principles. These early colonists had no way of knowing just how uninhabitable this land really was. By 1804 the first settlers' eager anticipation had vanished into the mist.

Despite difficult circumstances, many newcomers laboured to create a new life here. One determined soul was John McDonald. Around 1804 he and his wife built a sturdy frame house. For a short time John and his beloved lived in peace and soon heard the pit-a-pat of little feet. It was, however, a short-lived dream. A series of mysterious persecutions began. John and his family did not live in isolation — a very unusual family resided close by. Others in the area referred to this family as the people of the long, low, log house; they were a family that consisted of an old woman, her two sons, and one daughter. They were somewhat reclusive and unsociable people with few associations in their community.

The land of John McDonald had been coveted by the people of the long, low, log house. They approached him on several occasions with offers of purchase, but John always refused. (Was this decision connected to all the mysteries he and his family encountered?)

In those days the wives wove homespun cloth for clothing and straw into hats for protection from the blazing sun. These were shared activities among the settlers. One fine day while the men were occupied with farm duties, the young women gathered at the McDonald barn to pick and prepare straw for an afternoon of hat-making. The barn was built of logs and inside it were poles that stretched from side to side overhead, forming hangers for the flax.

As the women sat chatting and working, they were startled by the sudden plunge of one of the flax poles overhead. Although the pole fell right in their midst, it struck no one. Then a second of these poles crashed, and a third! The ladies fled to the house. No sooner were they inside than there was the crash of glass and a lead bullet lay at their feet, then another, and finally a shower of bullets came and the young women fled the house. There were no explanations for this.

For a few days all was peaceful on the McDonald farm. Then, one evening close to midnight, John was awakened by the sound of marching men, moving backwards and forwards with measured steps, then stillness, then more heavy tramping, but no one was to be seen. For three successive years many unexplainable manifestations afflicted the McDonald family.

Bullets through the windows became almost a daily occurrence. John finally barricaded the windows with heavy boards. The bullets passed through the wood, without leaving a mark! By this time the whole countryside was aware, alert and alarmed.

John McDonald was really beside himself. He and his family were anxious and tense from this relentless activity. They had been haunted by noises in the night, cups and saucers flying through the air, and their house was even reported to rise at one end or the other by as much as one metre (three feet).

An officer in the British army, Captain Lewis Bennett, visited Baldoon specifically to meet with the McDonald family and examine the situation. During his visit Bennett's own gun exploded for no apparent reason, and he witnessed the hauntings first-hand. One incident involved a baby in a cradle who suddenly began to scream as though in pain. She could not be consoled, but when picked up, a hot stone was discovered beneath the blankets. When the stone was removed another appeared. This was repeated several times. Little balls of fire were seen floating in mid-air and settling in various parts of the house. Every room in the house experienced this kind of fire.

The hauntings began to intensify. McDonald was exhausted and desperate. The family was not safe. Then one day flames burst out in a dozen places simultaneously and, although the family escaped, all was burned and lost.

John and his family moved to the safety of his father's house, and life seemed to return to normal. But it was not over. Once more the fearful tramping started, day and night; the furniture moved about, and a heavy kitchen cupboard fell to the floor with a thud. McDonald sought help this time from one Reverend McDorman. He was different, at least for a man of the cloth — he acknowledged the dark side. McDorman told McDonald that he knew a doctor's daughter who had the gift of second sight and the mystical power to do stone readings. John implored the reverend to take him to her. They travelled together for several days to see her. John told the young girl of the many mysterious happenings.

She listened intently and asked, "Did you ever have any trouble about a piece of land?"

"Not exactly trouble," replied John.

"Did one of your neighbours desire to purchase a portion of your land and did you refuse?" asked the girl.

McDonald nodded.

The girl replied, "People in a long, low, log house?"

McDonald said, "Yes."

Turning to her stone, the girl remained in a trance-like state for some time. Eventually, she asked, "Have you seen a stray black goose in your flock?"

"Yes," he replied.

She continued, "In that bird lives the destroyer of your peace. It has taken the shape of a bird and it is your enemy. You shall mould a bullet of sterling silver and fire it at the bird. If you wound it, your enemy shall be wounded in some corresponding part of their body. Go and be at peace."

Upon his return McDonald did as the young girl said. He and a party of men located a flock of geese by the river. He drew a bead on the black goose in the flock. The strange bird cried out like a human when it was wounded and made its way to the reeds with a broken wing.

Determinedly, John turned his footsteps toward the marsh, where the long, low, log house stood. One anxious look revealed all. There sat the old woman resting in a chair — and she had a broken arm. When she saw him, she pulled back.

For John McDonald and his family, no spiritual manifestations were ever seen or heard of again. Fact, it would seem, is truly stranger than fiction.

Bancroft

They call it Eagle's Nest, a sacred place once worshipped by those who paddled the York River and lived in harmony with nature. The land was clothed in pine, the ground covered in a rich brown carpet of needles that felt only the soft tread of a moccasined foot. The passage of time gave witness to the loss of peace once found here, at this eagle's cliff, as the settlers' axes hewed the town of Bancroft.

In the northern part of Hastings County at the junction of Highway 28 and 62, approximately 104 kilometres (65 miles) northeast of Peterborough and 20 kilometres (12 miles) northwest of Belleville, is the town of Bancroft. It was originally named York Mills, because of the potential of the river, and then York River when the first post office was opened, May 1, 1861.

Although the history of the district of Bancroft does not start until the 1850s, Hastings County was in the news as far back as 1792. It was Governor Simcoe who proclaimed that Upper Canada would be divided into 19 counties; the 11th one was Hastings. This name was chosen in honour of the family of Francis Rawdon-Hastings (1754–1826), a military leader and distinguished soldier during the American Revolution. His family took their name from the town of Hastings in Sussex, England. Francis Rawdon-Hastings became the marquis of Hastings in 1817.

In order to settle Hastings County, officials needed to negotiate the right to the ownership of the land with the Natives. On November 5, 1818, Chief Pahtosh, the leader of the Chippewas in the area, along

BANCROFT, ONT.

The main street of Bancroft circa 1915.

with other Native leaders, met with government officials to discuss the surrender of their territory. They agreed to surrender 1,951,000 acres of land to the government.

For the sale of this land the treaty read, "Every Native man, woman and child will receive the amount of 10 dollars in goods at the Montreal prices, so long as such man, woman or child shall live, but such annuity will cease and be discounted to be paid in right of any individual who may have died between the respective periods of payment, and the several individuals then living, only, shall be considered as entitled to receive the yearly payment of 10 dollars in goods as above stated."

The Native families diminished over the years until their paths in the forest were no longer visible and their sacred sites were lost to view.

The first white settlers to arrive in the area were the Clarks, in 1853. Tragedy knocked at their door when the wife and daughter drowned in the river at the mouth of the creek that now flows under Highway 62. This creek was later named Clark Creek in honour of Bancroft's first family of settlers.

In the spring of 1855, hard on the heels of the first surveyor, two young Englishmen arrived, James Cleak and Alfred Barker. They were educated men, ready and willing to test their skills in this harsh new country. Cleak opened a store and became the first postmaster, but Barker's fate remains unrecorded. Other early settlers included Henry Gaebel, Philip Harding, Thomas Sparrow, Patrick Kavanagh, the Vances, the Siddons, and the Sweets.

The construction of Monck Road, named in honour of Governor-General Lord Monck, began in 1866. The road started at Lake Couchiching and proceeded east to the Rideau Lakes. Although it was primarily built to open up the back woods of Upper Canada, it also served as a military trail. The Monck Road played a very strategic role in the settlement of York River, since it, along with the Hastings and the Mississippi Colonization roads, brought more settlers to the northern townships of the country. By 1868 York River's population had swelled to 89 families.

It wasn't long before the lumberjacks arrived to harvest the large stands of virgin forest. A lumber company, named Bronson and Weston, set up headquarters just east of present-day Bancroft. This company brought in hundreds of teams of horses to draw logs. In time, the Gilmour Lumber Company, the Rathburn Company, and the Eddy Company all worked limits in the area. The crews often worked together on the drives which started as the ice broke up. Many a man was drowned. One such river driver was laid to rest where the traffic lights now blink at the junction of Hastings and Bridge Streets and, as was the custom of the day, his boots marked the spot.

When rival lumber crews converged in Bancroft, the "fur" would fly. Each group had a champion strongman and, of course, a fight was always in order. The rules were simple. Each man carried a large stone to be tossed, like a gauntlet, to begin the fight. Once begun, anything went, and they fought till one lay helpless on the ground. It was then the privilege, or perhaps the obligation, of the victor to rake the fallen man's face with his spiked boots and mark him for life as the beaten warrior. One assumes that the drink consumed during this revelry provided some anaesthetic benefits. Louie Brisette was one such river driver of long ago, who lost to a younger man, and was said to sport a heavy beard for the rest of his life.

By 1872, York River was beginning to take on the appearance of a permanent settlement, albeit a rowdy one, and often likened to the wild west. However rough, the lumber industry did assist the growth of the village and the commerce that came to support the necessities of life. A Methodist Church opened for worship, a doctor arrived in 1888, and Sarah Cooper arrived to offer her services as a teacher.

On October 15, 1879, the leading businessman of the community, Senator Billa Flint, changed the name of York River to Bancroft to honour his wife, Phoebe Bancroft.

Although gold was discovered by Marcus Herbert Powell south of the town on August 15, 1866, on John Richardson's farm in Eldorado, it wasn't until 1897 that Bancroft gained attention and fame for its mineral deposits. In October of that year, R. Bradshaw discovered free-surface gold and gold fever struck Bancroft. One of the biggest winners in the draw was Mrs. J.B. Cleak's chicken. One fine day in 1902 the bird was escorted to the chopping block and, strange as it seems, Mrs. Cleak discovered a gold nugget in the pullet's crop.

Bancroft became famous for its earth minerals. Because ancient glaciers had moved soil and rock to gradually expose the very heart of volcanic mountains, Bancroft was set to become the mineral capital of Canada. Approximately 1,600 minerals have been identified to date.

In 1960 a mineral society was formed and the first rock show was held. An annual Rockhound Gemboree was the result, and Canada's largest mineral and gem show is still held each year from Thursday to Sunday before the civic holiday Monday in August. People can discover minerals firsthand in the countryside by way of a guided mineral trip any Tuesday or Thursday during July and August.

Nevertheless, for many, the most historic and sacred site in Bancroft remains Eagle's Nest. It is a place of mystery and beauty. It was here that the great eagles nested and here that the Natives prayed. No one is quite sure when the eagles left. What *is* recorded is the incident of 1883. Screams from outdoors brought Mr. and Mrs. Gaebel outside to witness a great eagle trying to carry off a small child who had been playing. They attacked the eagle with a broom and rake before it finally gave up its prey. A decision was made by the Gaebels and their neighbours to rid the village of eagles. Eggs were removed from the nest, the eagles disappeared temporarily, and there were no sightings again until 1902. In January 1918, the *Bancroft Times* recorded that a young man named

Sararas had shot an eagle measuring two metres (six feet) from wing tip to wing tip. He displayed it at the butcher shop of the game warden, James McCaw, who attempted to sell it. In the 1930s the tree in which the eagles had nested toppled to the ground.

Nature is as rugged as ever in Bancroft and, with or without eagles at Eagle's Nest, the vista is beautiful and the minerals are as abundant as ever.

The Ray Monster
and the Shadow

Folklore, myths, and legends begin as traditional narratives, but over time, as they are told and retold, stories tend to become archetypes — symbols for the truths of our existence, the external and internal, our landscapes and ourselves.

To believe in these stories was to experience the symbolic power of the supernatural, which, contrary to much modern thought, was rife with knowledge and valuable lessons. These stories are still here with us. All you have to do is feel their truth … and see.

A ready connection our sacred landscape and the knowledge and power of life around us is through the stories of First Nations, particularly the stories passed down locally from our own early Natives.

"They [the Ojibwa Indians of Parry Island] lived much nearer to nature than most white men, and they looked with a different eye on the trees and the rocks, the water and the sky," wrote Diamond Jenness of the National Museum of Canada in 1929. "They were less materialistic, more spiritually minded, than Europeans, for they did not picture any great chasm separating mankind from the rest of creation, but interpreted everything around them in much the same terms as they interpreted their own selves."

While researching for his report, titled *The Ojibwa Indians of Parry Island, Their Social and Religious Life*, Jenness learned that —according to the Ojibwa — man consisted of three parts, a corporeal body (*wiyo*) that decays and disappears after death, a soul (*udjitchog*) that travels after death to the land of souls in the west, ruled by Nanibush, and a shadow (*udjibbom*) that roams about on earth but generally remains near the grave.

In Jenness's words, "The soul is located in the heart and is capable of travelling outside the body for brief periods, although if it remains separate too long the body will die ... The soul is the intelligent part of man's being. The soul is also the seat of the will."

The shadow is slightly more indefinite than the soul. It is located in the brain, but like the soul, the shadow often operates apart from the body. Jenness elaborates:

> In life, it [the shadow] is the 'eyes' of the soul, as it were, awakening the latter to perception and knowledge ... When a man is travelling, his shadow goes before or behind him. Normally it is in front, nearer to his destination. There are times when a man feels that someone is watching him, or is near him, although he can see no one, it is his shadow that is warning him, trying to awaken his soul to perceive the danger.

The shadow is invisible, but sometimes it allows itself to be seen with the same appearance as the body. This is why you often think you see someone who is actually miles away.

In 1929, Wasauksing (Parry Island) resident Francis Pegahmagabow shared this story about the shadow: "My two boys met me at the wharf yesterday evening and accompanied me to my house. Sometime before our arrival, my sister-in-law looked out of the window and saw the elder boy pass by. It was really his shadow that she saw, not the boy himself, for we must have been nearly a mile away at the time."

Many Ojibwa living on Parry Island in the 1920s still believed that all objects had life, and life was synonymous with power. Just as man's power comes from his intelligence, his soul, so does the power of the animal, the tree, and the stone.

Mr. Pegahmagabow explained, "Long ago the manidos or supernatural powers gathered somewhere and summoned a few Indians through dreams, giving them power to fly through the air to the meeting place ... The Indians [their souls] travelled thither, and the manidos taught them about the supernatural world and the powers they had received from the Great Spirit. Then, they sent the Indians home again."

The Parry Island Ojibwa found authority for their belief in a world of supernatural beings around them, beings who are part of the natural order of the universe no less than man himself, whom they resemble in the possession of intelligence and emotions. Like man, they too are male or female and in some cases have families of their own. Some are friendly to the Native peoples, others are hostile. According to the museum report of 1929, there are manidos everywhere, or there were until the white man came, for today, the Indians say, most of them have moved away.

According to Jenness, "Occasionally, the Parry Islanders speak of a Maji Manido. Bad Spirit, referring either to some lesser being malevolent to man, most commonly the great serpent or water spirit. Apparently, the chief enemies to man are the water-serpents, which can travel underground and steal away a man's soul. If lightning strikes a tree near a native person's wigwam it is the thunder-manido driving away some water-spirit that is stealing through the ground to attack the man or his family. The leader of all water-serpents is Nzagima."

One needed to be very careful to protect the soul, Jenness points out. "Until quite recently, and perhaps even now in certain families, adolescent boys and girls were compelled to fast for a period in order to obtain a vision and blessing from some manido," he noted. "Parents gave their children special warning against a visitation from the great serpent, which might appear to them in the form of a man and offer its aid and blessing. A boy or girl who dreamed they received a visit from a snake should reject its blessing and inform their father, who would bid their return and seek a second visitation, since the evil serpent never repeats its overtures once they have been rejected. If then, a snake appears in another dream the boy or girl may safely accept its blessing. But if he incautiously accepts a blessing from the evil serpent he will deeply rue it afterwards, for sooner or later he and his family will have to feed it with their souls and die."

John Manatuwaba, a 70-year-old Ojibwa in 1929, recalled a family who fed their souls to the serpent: "A Parry Island couple had three children, two boys who died very young and a child that died at birth. Two years ago the serpent swallowed the man's soul. The woman then confessed that in her girlhood she had accepted a blessing from the evil serpent."

"I recall the tales about the water-serpent," stated a First Nations resident of Parry Island today. "It was told to us to keep the kids from going out in deep water. This kept the children safe.

"I have heard that the water-serpent lives in Three Mile Lake and travels underground to Hay Bay. It was told to us that when a south wind blows and the water becomes murky the serpent is moving in the water."

According to another First Nations resident, a group of young children encountered the water spirit in the 1950s on Parry Island. The creature was snake-like and had legs. It could travel through the forest as well as the water.

One Native elder on the island, when asked about the water spirit, reinforced the belief that the creature is actually a spirit.

There are other spirits that inhabit the district, such as the little people called the Memegwesi. They are friendly manidos, or rather a band or family of manidos. They may play pranks on the people, but never harm them. In the early part of the last century, a Parry Island native on his way to Depot Harbour saw a Memegwesi going down a creek. It had the outline of a man, but only its face was visible, the body being concealed beneath a huge growth of whiskers.

John Manatuwaba, recalled this encounter with the Memegwesi: "At the north end of Parry Sound, in what white men call Split Rock Channel, there is a crag known to the Indians as Memegwesi's Crag. Some natives once set night lines there, but their trout were always stolen."

At last one of the men sat up all night to watch for the thief. At dawn he saw a stone boat manned by two Memegwesi approaching, one a woman, the other bearded like a monkey. The watcher awakened his companions and they pursued the stone boat, which turned around and called to the Indians, "Now you know who stole your trout. Whenever you want calmer weather give us some tobacco, for this is our home." The boat and its occupants then entered the crag and disappeared.

Jenness also discovered that there are two kinds of invisible Indians, both closely akin to manidos. "One kind has no name, the other is called bagudzinishinabe or 'Little Wild Indian.' To see an individual of either kind confers the blessing of attaining old age."

The bagudzinishinabe are dwarfs that do no harm, Jenness found, but play innumerable pranks on human beings. Though small, no larger in fact than a little child, they are immensely strong. Sometimes they shake the poles of a wigwam, or throw pebbles on its roof; or they steal a knife from a man's side and hide it in his lodge. Often a person will eat and eat and still feel unsatisfied. He wonders how he can eat so much and still be hungry, but the dwarfs, unseen, are stealing the food from his dish.

Occasionally, you hear the reports of their guns, but cannot see either the dwarfs or their tracks. Yet, Francis Pegahmagabow stated that he once saw their tracks, "like those of a tiny baby," on a muddy road on Parry Island. A few years ago a Native person camping on the island awoke in the morning to discover tiny, child-like tracks alongside her tent.

In 1976, a Rosseau area resident who was studying with Native elders encountered the little people.

"This one day I was in a beechnut forest south of Algonquin Park and I had stopped to eat some nuts," he said. "Afterwards I sat down in a glade near a babbling brook. I dozed off.

"Suddenly I woke up and caught a glimpse of a creature about 10 feet away. At that moment it ducked behind a tree. Both of us were surprised to see each other. Then another creature appeared in the distance followed by another one to my right. I had never seen such a creature in my life. They were short, approximately two feet tall. Short mousy brown hair covered their entire body. They stood upright on their hind legs. Their front legs were shorter. I recall their long rabbit-like ears that hung straight down their back. I had the feeling their ears could rise up like a rabbit in an alert position. The creature's eyes were set in the front of their face. The eyes were quite expressive. The nose was flat. They had no tail.

"They communicated telepathically, by way of images, leaving you with a solid impression.

"Then they led me over to the creek. They communicated that this was a special place for them. It was here that they would adjust the stones in the stream to create certain tones that would help them raise their consciousness. They told me that the lower the tone, the greater the level of consciousness.

"They communicated to me that they liked tobacco and to bring some the next time. Their favourite food was red squirrel." This was another tale of the Memegwesi.

In 2009 a radio special with a Cree elder was done on CBC about the Memegwesi. It is truly wonderful that these little-known creatures are being remembered.

These mysterious stories help to introduce the possibilities of seeing our world in a new way, to awaken us to the magic and enchantment lurking in all four directions, to engage our souls.

Here is a tradition, from those same Natives, to ponder. When you meet a person on the road, address them after you have passed them. Your soul and their soul will then continue on their separate ways and only your bodies and shadows will remain to converse. If there should be disagreement between you it will pass away quickly, and your souls will be unaffected.

Belleville

A crude log cabin on the banks of the Moira River near the Bay of Quinte was built by a fur trader named Asa Wallbridge. He is recorded as the first white settler in the area. Natives were known to have camped and hunted in the vicinity prior to his arrival; not far from the river's mouth was a Native burial ground.

Most communities were founded and developed by men, sometimes accompanied by women, but Belleville's beginnings relied on the strength and determination of two pioneer women. Captain George Singleton and Lieutenant Isaac Ferguson were United Empire Loyalists and, incidentally, brothers-in-law, who set up a fur trading post together with their wives in 1794. By 1789 the Singletons had a child. That same year, Singleton died while on route to Kingston for winter staple supplies, and Ferguson died shortly thereafter. The two women, with the child John to care for, carried on at the trading post alone. Fortunately, other settlers were not long in joining them. Captain John Walden Meyers was next and he brought enterprise with him — a gristmill on the Moira River. He added a sawmill, a trading post, and a distillery. Meyers also operated a brick kiln and in 1794 erected, on a hill overlooking the Moira, what is recorded to be the first brick house in Upper Canada.

It was this industrial base that quickly attracted other settlers, and a village soon appeared below the mill at the river's mouth. The settlement became known as Meyers' Creek. In 1816, the village was 48 houses strong, officially surveyed by Samuel G. Wilmot, and a post office was opened. The village was then given the name Belleville. The name came from Lady Arabella (Bella) Gore, wife of the provincial lieutenant-governor Francis Gore, who visited there that same year.

In 1836 Belleville was incorporated as a police village, and Billa Flint, a local businessman, was elected as the first president of the Board of Police. Belleville was a rapidly developing lumber centre and became a town in 1850. Flint had been successful in organizing a temperance society, and as a merchant he was responsible for erecting extensive wharves and storehouses, not to mention Flint's sawmill. Billa Flint, in a letter to the editor of the *Weekly Intelligencer* in 1879, described Belleville as it was in 1829:

"Fifty years ago, I arrived in Belleville on the steamer, Sir James Kent. Fifty years ago, there was not one foot of sidewalk in town, not a drain to carry off the surplus water, and but one bridge, and that a poor one, over the river on Bridge Street. Fifty years ago, there were but two two-storey brick houses and both burned long ago. Fifty years ago, there was one dilapidated schoolhouse with a large mudhole in front all through the rainy season. There were no brick buildings on Front Street, and of the wooden ones only three showed of white and one of yellow paint."

In 1857 the Belleville Seminary, founded by the Methodist Episcopalian Church as a centre for higher Christian education, was opened. In 1866 it was named Albert College and became a university, with the full authority to grant degrees, in 1867. The women's school was called Alexander College. In 1884 the College reverted to a secondary school and was finally destroyed by fire in 1917. A new Gothic stone structure replaced it.

Another educational establishment to open in Belleville was the Ontario Business College, established in 1865, attended by students from far and wide. Lieutenant Governor Howland opened a provincial school for deaf children in 1870. Known today as Sir James Whitney School, it has become one of the largest and best institutes of its kind in North America.

On January 1, 1878, the village was incorporated as a city. The population was greater than 11,000, and Alexander Robertson served as the city's first mayor.

Archives of Ontario

Belleville has experienced several floods in the past century during spring breakup.

Belleville experienced the great flood of 1866, the worst one in the city's history. Hundreds of families living on both sides of the river were forced to abandon their homes. The lower section of the city, known as Sawdust Flats, suffered the greatest damage. The water took several days to subside, and the streets of Belleville were covered with debris, ice, and driftwood.

A similar disaster occurred on March 12, 1936, when, once again, the Moira River overflowed. More than 60 acres were submerged and several days of rescue and salvage operations were necessary. Huge chunks of ice littered the streets and inventories were destroyed in the lower levels of businesses on Front Street.

Like many communities who ultimately exhausted their timber resources, Belleville's industry declined in the 1870s. Sawmills and lumber manufacturing plants closed down and it wasn't until the 1920s that new industries moved in. Finally, in the late 1940s, Belleville experienced a post-war economic boom.

Belleville is a quiet, modest town. Humble beginnings have given this place a gift. Two women alone in the wilderness with a child established a tradition of quiet strength. These are things that you can feel when you walk down Belleville's streets — peace and quiet, friendliness, a sense of history, and the permanence that comes from strength and determination.

Brighton

Mention Brighton, Ontario, and apples come to mind. This small community on the eastern shore of Lake Ontario, just 8 miles west of Trenton, is quite renowned for its apple industry.

The cultivation of apple trees for harvesting can be traced back to Italy some 200 years ago. Thirty known varieties were grown and eventually introduced into other countries. The seeds of European apples were brought to Ontario by French settlers in the early 17th century.

Have you ever heard of Johnny Appleseed?

The main character in this story was John Chapman, a farm lad, who attended a term or two at Harvard College and then headed west. As early as 1801, Johnny saw settlers crossing the Ohio River and constructing cabins in a fertile wilderness; fertile, maybe, but devoid of fruit trees. Legend says that he carried the word of the Bible and also carried apple seeds. Johnny planted nurseries by streams for the benefit of the settlers who would follow. Frontiersmen carried seed pouches he had given them, and with those seeds they planted orchards as far west as Iowa.

Shortly after 1776, United Empire Loyalists arrived in Upper Canada with seeds and seedlings already acclimatized in North America. It was a Scottish immigrant, John McIntosh, who introduced a superior apple to Ontario. McIntosh had left New York State to settle in Dundela, Ontario, where he transplanted 20 wild-apple seedlings. His wife, Hannah, tended to the orchard with loving care, especially one particular tree. The grandchildren noticed this and called the fruit of this special tree "Granny's apple."

Many of the apple varieties that the pioneers grew no longer exist. It was reported that in 1892 one could choose from more than 878 varieties of apples. For example, the Alexander apple was introduced into England from Russia in 1817. The Fameuse or Snow apple was grown in the Province of Quebec with seeds from France. The Golden Russett came from New York State. The Ontario (a Wagner and Spy cross) came from Paris, Ontario, and the early Transparent from St. Petersburg.

In 1853, the average size of a farm in Brighton was 100 acres. Pioneer families raised cows and chickens and grew grain. Their apple orchards were usually located close to their buildings. Most of the yield from the orchard was used by the family. The apples that were dried over the kitchen stove were often taken to the general store and bartered for other goods.

Brighton's first settler was a United Empire Loyalist by the name of Obediah Simpson, who arrived there in 1796. There were other Loyalist families who followed him and many immigrants from the British Isles. They called their community Singleton's Corners.

When a road was built from York (Toronto) to Kingston in 1816, Singleton's Corners began to grow. John Kemp opened the first store, and John Singleton took the job of postmaster for the locality. The name of the community was later changed to Brighton.

By 1850 the first doctor arrived to serve the population of 500. A small schoolhouse was opened on Main Street and the first newspaper, the *Brighton Sentinel*, was published on February 23, 1853, by Alexander Begg, a settler from Scotland. One of the early issues of the paper contained a feature article on how to restore an old orchard. The writer recommended putting lime and manure around the trees and growing corn and potatoes under them. It also described how to prune to open up the centre of the apple tree and how to graft new varieties on existing trees.

Two other papers would follow: the *Brighton Weekly Flag* in 1855 and the *Brighton Ensign* in 1870. Brighton was incorporated as a village on March 24, 1859.

In 1853 H. Ganetsee established a commercial nursery, which had apple, cherry, and other fruit trees for sale. The first apple orchard, 3.2 kilometres (two miles) east of Brighton, was established with seeds brought from New York State in the early 1830s by Mr. John F. Sherman.

John Sherman was a blacksmith by trade, and worked in the villages of Warkworth and Brighton until 1845, when he chose to settle on a farm east of Brighton and plant his first orchard. Frederick W. Sherman was the last member of that family to operate an orchard on the property. When he died in March 1964, the orchards were sold, and the land was used for other purposes.

In the early days, Brighton needed a lawyer to oversee commerce. John Eyre was that ambitious man. Eyre assisted in founding the Union Agricultural Joint Stock Company at Clark's Hotel in 1873 and served one term as a member of Parliament. Circa 1880, he built a magnificent three-storey Georgian house, complete with a full basement, triple brick walls, open porches to the east and west sides, and turreted tower. This home, situated on Highway 2 just west of the village, would one day be called the Whitehouse.

When Eyre died in 1889, nine years after building his home, it seemed no one in the family wished to keep his pride and joy, and the house passed into the hands of a trust company until 1898, when Samuel Nesbitt, a grocer in Brighton, bought it.

Nesbitt was both industrious and highly imaginative. He founded the Brighton Bicycle Club on May 15, 1896, in the back of his dry goods store.

On April 24, 1896, he wrote the column "Bicycle" for the *Brighton Ensign* newspaper. Partly a sales announcement, it stated, "Ladies and gentlemen, I carry the largest stock of wheels in the country. I have selected these wheels that have given the best satisfaction in Canada and the United States." He later mentioned the names of people to whom he had sold wheels. On the list was Eleanor Bibby, a young lady who was soon to become his wife.

Nellie, as she was called, was described as a being a very proper Victorian lady, somewhat severe in appearance but motherly by nature. Samuel and Nellie raised two daughters, Frances and Edith, and two sons, Edwin and Ernest. In the 1920s Samuel renovated the Whitehouse, putting stucco on the outside of the building and constructing a tower with windows to overlook his 53 acres. It was said that Samuel enjoyed playing a game or two of cards in that tower. Between games he would watch his work hands in the field with the aid of binoculars.

Samuel's greatest contribution to Brighton and the country was a canning factory, which he established in 1894 under the auspices of Dominion Canneries. Being a progressive man, he also established a laboratory for the development of better quality fruits and of finer methods of canning. This included some experimental work concerning the preservation of foods. An article appeared in the paper on December 2, 1898, regarding apples stored in Brighton. It read, "Nearly 70,000 barrels of apples have been stored in Brighton to be repacked for shipment, principally to Liverpool, England and Glasgow, Scotland. During the last of October and November, 266 rail cars have been unloaded and stored in Mr. Sam Nesbitt's storehouses alone, and nearly 135 in other places in the town. There has been paid, for freight on apples inward here, the sum of $17,300. It has been stated that Mr. S. Nesbitt's facilities for storing apples in frost-proof storehouses exceeds that of any other town between Toronto and Montreal."

Nellie died in 1929 and Samuel, aged 69, married her younger sister, Maria, a French teacher at the teacher's college in Toronto. Samuel died in 1938 and the Whitehouse, known then as Grandfather's House, became Rene's Whitehouse Hotel. Rene was Irene Dickson's nickname. She managed the Nesbitt estate for the next 34 years, serving many celebrities at the hotel, among them Prime Minister William Lyon Mackenzie King, Mr. and Mrs. Walt Disney, and Irene Castle, the famous ballroom dancer. Today, the Whitehouse has been converted back to a residential home.

Anyone who has ever picked apples knows something about exercise and fresh air. In the early days, apple pickers would rise at 6:00 a.m. to have breakfast and then assemble at the farm before going out to the orchard. Pickers were expected to climb the first tree by 7:00 a.m., while it was still a bit dark and possibly cold. Everyone would stop at noon for a cold lunch and then return to work until 6:00 p.m. The grower would supply the picker with a ladder and a basket. Keep in mind that some of these trees were 80 years old and 40 feet high. In 1933 pickers were paid $1.50 a day.

There was a fair amount of rivalry among the picking gangs to see who could ship the most barrels per day. Around 1908, eight men working for Mr. Bradd picked and packed 109 barrels of Wagners in a 10-hour day. George DeLong and his gang of five men picked and packed 120 barrels of Starks in one day.

In the 1880s Brighton's industrial centre featured a carriage and sleigh factory and some farm equipment factories. Mr. Robinson operated an apple evaporator, while William Butler operated a sawmill. A harness shop was run by Robert Marshall. Brighton had its own cheese factory located on Cedar Street. The village was also known for the Brighton Nightwear Company, which manufactured pyjamas.

Every village, town, or city has had its occasional setback, and Brighton is no exception. The harsh winter of 1933–34 caused tremendous damage to Brighton's apple orchards. Brighton experienced 20 degrees of frost on October 24. This was followed by temperatures as low as -35 degrees Fahrenheit in December and January, 1934. The apples were frozen on the trees. An extremely dry summer was followed by a wet fall that prevented the apple tree wood from hardening properly. The leaves remained on the trees throughout the winter. Those trees which had borne heavily died, while those without a crop survived. The older varieties such as Cooper's market, Gano, Ben Davis, and Stark disappeared. The farmers were now faced with replanting and many growers chose the Melba, Lobo, McIntosh, and Cortland varieties. Other farmers decided to end their apple business entirely. Brighton then saw houses where the old orchards had once stood.

In July 1975 the Downtown Business Association made the decision to hold a fall festival. They called it Brighton's Applefest. Their first Applefest hosted a street fair for one day. When the coffee and baked goods ran out, the fair was over. The next year a few booths appeared. By 1977 the Lions, Legion, and Kinsmen Clubs assisted in Applefest. Today, Applefest is a four-day event attended by tourists from all over the province.

The success of Brighton as a community and a tourist destination is in part due to their long-standing heritage and traditions, much of which involves the growing of apples. Perhaps Brighton was able to get by without a doctor for as long as it did, until it had 500 residents, because, as the saying goes, "An apple a day ..."

Burlington

He was called Thayendanegea. In Mohawk it meant "two sticks tied together for strength." His English name was Chief Joseph Brant. A man of the Kamenhekaka nation, in 1798 he was granted 3,450 acres of land in Burlington by King George III, for his service to the Crown during the Seven Year War and the American Revolutionary War. This parcel of land included the area where the hospital and the museum, which both bear his name, are located.

Joseph Brant was born in 1742 on the banks of the Ohio River during a hunting trip. He was raised in a place called Canajoharie, in the valley of the Mohawk River, in what is now New York State.

His Majesty's representative for Indian Affairs in the colony of New York was William Johnson. It is said that Johnson, while participating in a regimental muster, was approached by a 16-year-old girl, who asked if she could ride behind him on his horse. Thinking she was joking, he agreed. Suddenly, she leapt onto the saddle behind him and the two raced across the field. The girl was Molly Brant, Joseph's sister. William Johnson later married her and became his third wife.

During the Seven Years' War between France and England (1756–1763), Major General William Johnson appealed to his Native friends for assistance in fighting the French. Joseph Brant, aged 13, joined with other Mohawks to defeat the French. Johnson was later knighted Sir William Johnson.

At the age of 19, Joseph Brant was sent by Johnson to Moore's Charity School in Lebanon, Connecticut. The main mission of this college was to teach Natives to abandon their Native environment, mix with non-native students, learn English, and become missionaries among their own people. Joseph excelled in the two years he attended. Some historians believe that this was where he was converted to Christianity.

Upon his return he married Christine, the daughter of an Oneida chief, and together they resided in a frame house. Although they had two children, Christine died young of consumption in 1771; Brant married Susannah, who also died of consumption two years later; he was married a third and final time, to a woman named Catherine.

In 1776 war broke out between Britain and the American colonies. A year later at Oswego, a Council of the Six Nations was held with officers of the British Indian Department. A Treaty of Alliance was agreed upon and the Natives joined in the service of the King. For the next several years, Joseph Brant fought the American colonists from the Hudson River to the Ohio River in the Mohawk Valley. In 1779 Major General Sullivan, in command of the American troops, attacked the Native villages of the Mohawk Valley. He and his troops destroyed 41 Iroquois towns and left thousands of homeless Natives.

During a raid near Detroit, Brant developed a fever, which he treated in a traditional way. He went to a hill known to have rattlesnakes. There he waited for one to crawl out to sun itself. He caught the snake and took it to his camp, where he boiled it in water to make a broth. After drinking the soup he recovered quickly.

A peace treaty was signed in 1782 between England and the new United States. Without a territory to call their own, the Six Nations of the Iroquois looked to American and British governments for some assistance. Chief Brant chose to come to Canada with the British. The British assisted the Mohawks and other Iroquoian nations by giving them a tract of land on the Bay of Quinte and a further purchase of land on the Grand River, 10 kilometres (six miles) on each side of the river from its mouth to its source. The Natives then had property but no longer had possessions. Consequently, Brant went to England in 1786 to adjust the claims of his nation for their service during the war.

Land ownership became an issue of confusion and misunderstanding. The major problem concerned the right of Natives to dispose of their land as they wished. The government contended that the land had been given to the Natives in trust, for their own use only, and that no property could be disposed of without official approval. Joseph Brant believed that the Natives were a distinct nation able to enter into agreement on its own with individuals or sovereign states. He had no problem with selling or leasing land to non-natives to create an income. Some Natives, themselves, had concerns over the dispensation of the money. In the long run, land ownership came to an end in 1841. Samuel Jarvis, Indian superintendent, decided that the only way to prevent white settlers from intruding was to surrender the land to the Crown to be administered for the sole benefit of the Natives.

Joseph Brant, with his 3,450 acres of land, built a two-storey house out of timber brought by water from Kingston in 1800. He chose a site at Head-of-the-Lake overlooking both the bay and the lake. Joseph and Catherine were the first citizens of the present City of Burlington. On November 24, 1807, Joseph Brant died in his home at the age of 60. His body was removed to Six Nations land near Brantford. The location of his gravesite is not public knowledge.

One great tragedy from which Joseph Brant never fully recovered was the death of his eldest son Isaac. He was a young man with a fierce temper and was often under the influence of alcohol. During one of his drinking bouts he had an argument with his father. They came to blows. Tragically, during the fight Isaac suffered a head wound which later became infected and caused his death. Brant turned himself in to the authorities and asked to be tried in a court of law. He was found not guilty of the crime.

The earliest recorded settler on the site of the present-day city of Burlington was August Bates, who arrived in 1800. Joseph Brant at that time was selling land to his Loyalist friends, such as Nicholas Kern, who purchased 200 acres; Robert Wilson, who bought 211 acres; and Thomas Ghent, who acquired farmland from Brant in 1805. A community began to develop around the Brant homestead.

Shortly after Brant's death in 1807, James Gage purchased 338 acres of land, where he erected a mill and other commercial establishments. By 1817, 16 dwellings stood in the hamlet, which they called Wellington Square in honour of the Duke of Wellington. In 1826, a post office was opened.

The construction of wharves, warehouses, and a large flour mill helped to create a busy centre of commerce. By 1845, 400 inhabitants called Wellington Square home. Wheat became a major export commodity of the area. Dozens of schooners anchored in the busy harbour, and on some days long lines of carts drawn by horse or oxen would be waiting on the shore to unload the grain. Shipbuilding also became a major industry in the settlement. At one time 17 sawmills operated in the area, and by mid-century Wellington Square boasted a tannery, a pottery, two wagon makers, a foundry, and several general stores.

Meanwhile, Port Nelson on the lakeshore, located at the bottom of what is now the Guelph Line, had also become an important and busy shipping point. In 1873 the hamlets of Wellington Square and Port Nelson amalgamated, becoming the village of Burlington. The name came about as a distortion or variation of the name Bridlington, a town in Yorkshire, England.

By 1913 Burlington had its own coat-of-arms, designed by Miss Arial Shapland. The village had, by then, annexed some of the adjoining territories and became a town in December, 1914.

In 1937 construction of the Joseph Brant Museum was underway on the original site of Brant's home near the shoreline of Lake Ontario. It was and still is a replica of Brant's abode. Today, inside the museum, visitors can experience four galleries that exhibit artifacts relating to the life of Joseph Brant, the history of Burlington, traditional Iroquoian life, and Canadian costume. The museum also has an impressive reference library on the same subjects.

In 1958 the amalgamation of Burlington, Nelson Township, and a part of East Flamborough Township helped to create a new and much larger town of Burlington. At one time it was known as the largest town in Ontario. It was allowed to retain town status because of its relative lack of industry. The Burlington Skyway was officially opened in 1958, and at that time it was the largest bridge ever to have been constructed by the Ontario Department of Highways. The centre span of the bridge is 36 metres (120 feet) above the harbour entrance and the bridge is 7 kilometres (4.37 miles) long.

Burlington achieved city status on January 1, 1974. Since that time, it has seen a steady flow of progress and development.

BRANT HOUSE BURLINGTON ONT

Archives of Ontario

Across the road from the Joseph Brant Museum stood the Brant House, a famous hotel and dance hall on the shores of Lake Ontario.

It does seem ironic that although this was Joseph Brant's first home, and although he was generous to subsequent settlers, and despite the fact that many Ontario towns reflect their native roots through their names, there is no connection made to Joseph Brant in the name of Burlington.

Cobalt

On a fall day in 1903, blacksmith Fred LaRose of Cobalt worked more than a horseshoe with his hammer. According to local lore, Fred threw his hammer at what he thought were the glimmering eyes of a curious fox peeking at him from behind a rock and instead struck a vein of silver.

Earlier that year two lumbermen, J.H. McKinley and Earnest Darragh, were exploring the timber limits when they spotted metallic flakes in the rock at the south end of Long Lake. The men extracted some samples and sent them away to be analyzed. The results specified silver values of 4,000 ounces to the ton.

The site was staked on August 4, 1903.

This discovery was to spark one of the richest silver booms Canada had ever seen. It gave rise to many additional discoveries that ultimately became a billion-dollar Canadian mining industry.

News of the discovery of silver brought Dr. Willet G. Miller, Ontario's first provincial geologist, to the site. He soon set up a sign beside the railway tracks that read COBALT STATION.

A mining rush was on and people from around the world came to reap their share of the riches. By 1910 the silver production of Cobalt ranked fourth in the world. The mining industry, comprised of more than 100 mines, eventually produced 333,419,562 ounces of silver at an average price of 58.95 cents an ounce.

In 1911 the population of Cobalt and surrounding area had reached 13,000. A year later the town was incorporated, but no one envisioned the mining rush lasting more than a few years, and as a result the town was built up in a haphazard manner on the west side of Cobalt Lake. The business district of the community provided goods and services to the prospectors and mining companies who purchased land around and under the townsite. The settlers were treated as squatters, because civic and social needs were not to interfere with mineral exploration. A resident of Cobalt could be evicted from their home, at any time, if a silver vein was discovered beneath their house.

By then the town featured 18 hotels that catered to visitors and employees of the mines; four banks serviced the financial needs of the mining industry; and six churches, two schools, a courthouse and jail rounded out the public services. The development of the town attracted a broad cross-section of people. British and French immigrants made up the basic business core and the miners were primarily of central and eastern European descent.

Cobalt, like any other town, was not without misfortune. Its first disaster occurred in May 1906 when tons of dynamite exploded, causing a fire which destroyed a large section of the town. This was the first of what was to be many fires to besiege this small community. In July 1909, another fire left 3,000 people without homes.

The spring of 1907 was remembered for an epidemic of smallpox that claimed the lives of many, including Dr. William Henry Drummond, the famous habitant poet. After helping to fight the disease for many long days and nights, the doctor died in his sleep at his home at the Drummond Mine site east of Cobalt. A cairn, dedicated to the memory of the poet, still stands today on the site of his home. In 1918 an outbreak of influenza claimed more lives.

By the 1920s the price of silver had dropped sharply, many mines were closed, and still others ran dry. The community itself declined drastically during the Depression of the 1930s, but a strong band of those pioneer miners and their descendants have remained to keep the heart of Cobalt beating.

In 1953 a group of dedicated citizens decided to preserve the rich heritage of the area. Cobalt's Northern Ontario Mining Museum opened in 1961 to feature one of the country's finest silver collections, not to mention photographs, artifacts, and memorabilia from the earliest days of Cobalt. In 1985 the Cobalt Historical Society created the Heritage Silver Trail, a self-guided tour through the back roads of the Cobalt

The town of Cobalt as it appeared circa 1908.

camp. Visitors travel to various sites, which focus on different aspects of mining. Each site features history and information signs, as well as photographs, encouraging one to relive the great silver rush of 1903 and experience the exciting history of this mining camp. A travel guidebook is also available at the museum.

For those who are up for some exercise, the walking tours of Cobalt feature all-day activities that help you to discover a century of living. The tours begin at the museum on Silver Street, where the story of the mining is told in 7 galleries — the story that made the once-booming community of Cobalt famous.

After touring the museum, you walk left along Silver Street to the Classic Theatre. Built in the 1920s, the theatre was the last of a string of live vaudeville theatres that operated in the early years of Cobalt; restored in 1993, the building is now a state-of-the-art live theatre once again.

The next stop is the Royal Exchange Building. Built in 1909, this is now the site of the Fraser Hotel, one of Cobalt's most impressive buildings. It was fitted with special fireproof doors on the upstairs suites and boasted a purple-mauve glass sidewalk that was lit from underneath. During the 1930s it served as a beer parlour.

On Prospect Street you come to the oldest structure on the street: The Bank of Commerce. Cobalt's first bank actually opened in a tent on August 9, 1905. It is said that paydays were so busy at the Bank of Commerce that the manager would remove the windows so the miners could climb through to be served.

The town square is the next site, located at the corner of Prospect and Argentite Street. This was the central meeting place in Cobalt. Arriving settlers would leave the train station, climb the hill to the square, and fan out in search of vacant land.

Argentite Street was actually called Swamp Street at one time because the sludge from the Coniagas Mill located at the bottom of the hill often flowed onto the street.

The section of land down the hill towards the arena was once called Pigtown. (The Nipissing Central Railway operated regular streetcar service down into Pigtown, carrying shoppers, residents, and miners.) Cobalt boasted other neighbourhoods too — Fintown, Frenchtown, and squatter communities around the mining sites.

The Cobalt arena is on the tour as well. This was where the Coniagas Mine was located, on the hill behind the arena. You can still see the ruins of this operation.

Back up toward Silver Street is the site of the Fire Station. Fire was a nightmare for townspeople. Numerous fires have destroyed the buildings, ruined livelihoods, and killed residents. Many of the early structures were built quickly with any available material, including old dynamite boxes; they were tinderboxes waiting to go up in smoke.

Farther down Silver Street you will come to the Coniagas #4 mining shaft. This is one of the most unique buildings in Cobalt. The mining company sank a shaft here in 1914, even though it was right in the centre of the downtown. The shaft was sunk to a depth of 350 feet (100 metres). A cage, which was used to transport four men down the shaft, is still in the building. After the mining company left Cobalt, the building served as a grocery store. The owner relied on the cold underground air to keep his meat cool.

Today, Cobalt no longer represents the mining boom of 1903. Gone are the surplus of hotels and the prospectors who filled them. What remains is a small historic community struggling to survive the changing times.

Cobourg

amuel Ash of New York State arrived at Kingston in 1797, after
travelling across Lake Ontario in an open boat with his father and his
brother-in-law. Their first purchase was two oxen, and then they headed
west where they heard there was land. They found 200 acres that took
their fancy and settled in to clear it. Low, wet, and somewhat swampy,
with great meandering creeks that wound their way to Lake Ontario, this
terrain would be transformed by visionaries and dreamers into a town
called Cobourg.

Among the many privations from which the settlers suffered, one
of the greatest was the lack of footwear. Mr. Ash would tell in later years
how he sometimes came home from work in the evening to find his wife
absent. He would know that she had gone in search of the cows, which
were in the habit of straying into the woods. He would then set out to
look for her, in the knowledge that he could find her by tracing the marks
of her bleeding feet on the stones and brush as she went along.

Eluid Nickerson came next. The following year, 1798, he built a
log home near the present-day King and Division business section
of town. Elijah Buck arrived in 1808 and he, too, accumulated a large
tract of land and promptly opened a tavern. The settlement became
known as Buckville until the name was changed to Amherst, and then
to Hamilton, after the township in which it was situated. In 1819 the
village was renamed Cobourg in honour of the marriage of Princess
Charlotte to Prince Leopold of Saxe-Coburg, Germany. The extra *o* crept
in, presumably through ignorance of the correct spelling.

In 1827 Cobourg had about 40 houses, two inns, four stores, several distilleries, a gristmill, and a population of 350. There was still no harbour, but plans for one were underway and there was talk of a railway from Cobourg to Rice Lake and Peterborough.

The 1830s saw the beginning of a massive wave of immigrants. Cobourg had its new harbour by then, and it offered both rich and poor the opportunity to settle. By 1847, 5,393 immigrants had landed here. The citizens of Cobourg felt that their community was destined to be a city of greatness one day. The harbour and proposed railway to Peterborough were expected to bring great prosperity. Cobourg's residents even hired a noted Toronto architect, Kivas Tully, to design a town hall.

Excavation and construction of the town hall was underway by 1856. Three years later Victoria Hall was almost completed. The local newspaper, the *Star*, described the interior of the building by stating, "As you enter, a spacious outer court presents itself to the chastely decorated Hall of Justice, the south wall of which has been tastefully painted with the Royal Arms in the centre, without color, and as though the whole were a piece of sculpture. The whole of the woodwork has been painted and grained in a superior manner under the superintendence of Mr. Hayden, who took the contract for painting the hall. Carpets have been laid down and stoves erected in the rooms required for use at the assizes … Too much praise cannot be given to all parties." On September 7, 1860, the Prince of Wales (later King Edward VII) arrived by boat at 9:30 p.m. and officially opened Victoria Hall.

The townspeople, fired with zeal to expand, obtained a charter to build a railway from Cobourg to Peterborough. On February 9, 1853, the first sod was turned near the corner of University Avenue and Railroad Street.

In the past, officials had considered a number of schemes to connect their town and Rice Lake, and, more particularly, Peterborough. In 1846 they had attempted to build a plank road to Gore's Landing, Rice Lake, but in only a few years the planks had split and rotted. The only solution, it seemed, was a railway.

The three-mile gap across Rice Lake would be spanned by a trestle. With dynamic enterprise the people of Cobourg voted to tax themselves to bring this railway into being. Peterborough offered no capital but plenty of encouragement.

The 15-mile line to Harwood on Rice Lake was completed by May, 1854. Meanwhile, a piling-machine had been pounding massive beams, for the trestle, into the muddy bottom of Rice Lake. On December 8th the first work-train arrived in Ashburnham, on the east side of the Otonabee River, opposite Peterborough.

The railway was a tremendous boon to the millers, merchants, and manufacturers of Peterborough. Cobourg's exports rose dramatically, and Harwood came to life as the main sawmill and shipping centre on Rice Lake.

There was, however, one significant problem: the impressive trestle bridge rested on shaky foundations and was soon no match for the winter ice on the lake. The ice pressure was quite capable of snapping a two-foot square beam in half. During the winter of 1854–55, the ice shoved some of the tresses, twisted the rails out of shape, and opened a two-metre (seven foot) gap at the Harwood end. Again and again, the bridge was closed for repairs. Any money the railway earned was soon spent on repairs to the teetering trestle bridge.

The bridge actually became quite an embarrassment when the Prince of Wales and his royal party, en route from Cobourg to Peterborough, in September 1860, had to be transferred from the train at Rice Lake to the steamer *Otonabee* for the lake crossing. Officials feared for the life of the prince if he were to cross the bridge by train. The train crept slowly across the rickety bridge, and the prince re-boarded on the other side. By the spring of 1862, the bridge finally collapsed and floated away with the ice. The demise of the bridge meant the demise of the entire Cobourg Railway.

In the early 1860s, Cobourg may have appeared to be a prosperous town, waiting to become a city, but the truth of the situation was far from its appearance. The local paper made continual reference to the hard times that had fallen on the town. The Cobourg and Peterborough Railway had cost a million dollars, yet it failed to pay running expenses. On May 13, 1864, Henry Hough wrote in the the *Cobourg World*, "It seems, as far as we can learn, to be generally admitted fact that Cobourg, as a business and commercial town, has gone down. There was a time when it took a front rank among the towns of the country; when business was brisk and plentiful; when the streets were thronged with bustling people, and the workshops with industrious and contented workmen." The citizens continued to pay for their town until 1938.

Archives of Ontario

The Commercial House, on the main street of Cobourg, in the 1870s.

In the 1870s Cobourg experienced the arrival of many Americans who were anxious to spend their summers by the lake. One American observed, on beholding the town hall, "That is indeed a splendid building, but where is the town for whose use it was built?"

At one time it was stated that every admiral in the American Navy had passed at least one holiday season in Cobourg. Society among them was very cultured and refined. Later on, a wealthier class of Americans, principally steel capitalists from Pittsburgh, arrived to make Cobourg their summer home. Some of these new arrivals purchased and enlarged stately old residences, while others erected palatial homes after the style of Newport, Maine.

General Charles Fitzhugh was one of the wealthy Americans who built a summer home in Cobourg. He was born in Oswego, New York, in 1838 and later entered West Point Academy. When the young men of the nation were called to war, Charles Fitzhugh at once gave his services to his country and, after being in action a short while, received a commission as first lieutenant. Promotion followed quickly in the field, and he soon became the youngest general in the northern army during the American Civil War.

This spacious mansion, entitled Strathmore and built in the 1870s, suited the period of elegance and grace created by the American summer homes in Cobourg.

He married Emma Shoenberger in 1865 and resigned from the army two years later. In 1900 he built Ravensworth, a stunning summer home on the shore of Lake Ontario. In keeping with the colonial appearance, the grounds were laid out in a graceful manner, with elegant gardens, immaculately groomed. Ravensworth was to become the scene of great family gatherings and marvelous social events for high, summer society. The architectural formality of the house complemented the lavish dinner parties, and the social rules were made palatable by the sweeping curves of gowns, the softly curled hair, the light laughter, and long gold cigarette holders. People flowed from one room to the other. Music and dancing continued until dawn, with crystal chandeliers glittering in the rays of the early morning sun.

Both the general and his wife died in 1923, and their summer home was sold to Richard Baylor Hickman of Kentucky. Soon after, Ravensworth became the scene of an attempted assassination. One evening Hickman was sitting in his library, quietly reading a book, when a bullet whistled through the air and lodged itself into the wall paneling three inches above his head. Hickman raced out of the house to search the grounds but was unable to find the culprit. He retired for the night, with the intention of notifying the police in the morning. Sometime during the night, the would-be assassin returned, entered the library, and removed the bullet from the wall. Neither bullet nor man were ever found.

Today, Ravensworth is a private residence and remains virtually unchanged. Still a splendid house, it is a reminder of a bygone era of ease and elegance.

Cobourg, over the years, has been home to several famous people. The first mayor, William Weller, established the widely known Weller Stage Line, operated from Montreal and Hamilton. Ulysses S. Grant, 18th president of the United States, spent his summers at Cobourg; Marie Dressler, a movie star perhaps best-known as Tugboat Annie, was born here. Others who once lived in Cobourg and went on to find fame elsewhere were James Cockburn, one of the Fathers of Confederation; Beatrice Lillie and Katharine Cornell, both famous actresses; and Paul Kane, the world-famous artist.

Cobourg may never have become a city, but the image of prosperity exemplified by Victoria Hall and other beautiful and unique period homes still remains. Thanks to those who persevered — the first settlers when they traced bleeding feet and lived in swampy land — we are able to enjoy the beauty carved out of this Ontario wilderness.

Cochrane

Francis Cochrane was the Ontario minister of lands, forests, and mines in the early 1900s. The townsite at the terminal point for the Temiskaming and Northern Ontario Railway was named in his honour.

The townsite itself was not laid out until 1907; prior to that, the area had been touched only by Natives, trappers, and the natural kingdom. In November 1907 a public sale of lots was held for prospective settlers. The lots measured 20 by 36 metres (66 by 120 feet), surrounded by 17 avenues 30 metres (100 feet) wide, running north and south, and narrower ones running east and west.

As you can well imagine, there were no long lineups to purchase these lots, as they were quite small for the standards of the time. The plans changed somewhat when lots were not properly cleared, and those not sold at the auction were allowed to keep their blankets of virgin forest. The close proximity of lots meant homes were built so close together that fire was a major threat to the community. As a matter of fact, Cochrane suffered a rash of fires in a span of six years.

A few months after its incorporation in 1910, Cochrane's core was destroyed in a burning blaze and promptly rebuilt. Later, in July 1911, at the height of the Porcupine gold rush, gale-force winds turned scattered bush fires into one massive firestorm that devastated several towns and mining camps in the area, including Cochrane and Timmins. The 3,000 residents of Cochrane rebuilt their town, hoping to never see the likes of such a fire again. Hopes aside, tragedy struck again, in July 1916. They called it "The Great Fire of 1916." High winds once again turned

Cochrane has survived a rash of fires and, as pictured, many heavy winters.

separate fires, which were already burning in the tinder-dry woods along the railway lines, into one vast conflagration that scorched 500,000 acres. Numerous settlements, including Matheson and Cochrane, were affected, and many lives were lost.

One of the first buildings in Cochrane was shipped on railway flat cars from its original site in Chapleau. The year was 1909 and the building was an Anglican Church. The church was set among the pine trees north of what was later known as Bishopthorpe. By 1914 there was also a Catholic Church and a Baptist Church.

The town underwent some changes after the fire of 1916. Residents opted for concrete foundations to beat the muskeg, and the streets in town were widened. By 1920 Cochrane had evolved from a frontier town into a prosperous centre. Although it was primarily a railway settlement, farming and lumbering had assumed important roles in the economics of the area. When prospectors discovered the minerals in the district, Cochrane quickly became a major supply and shipping point.

The town of Cochrane, located in the heart of excellent fishing and hunting country, is well-known to tourists. The popular Polar Bear Express conveys visitors on one-day train excursions in the summer, from Cochrane to the James Bay lowlands and the otherwise isolated communities of Moose Factory and Moosonee. The train operates from the end of June until Labour Day and offers the traveller a unique experience in northern sightseeing. Small planes, boats, and ski-doos can take you farther if you are keen to see more. A unique aspect to the train ride is that part of the track runs over bog land and involves a kind of "floating rail bed," which you can actually feel in the way it rides. You can also see first-hand the way folks who live in remote areas have to travel. Tiny, isolated settlements exist along the route, where people wait beside the track; the train simply stops for them if needed.

Looking at Cochrane another way, you could say, "It's at the end of the road!" It is well worth visiting, because that kind of existence creates quite a different town.

Creemore

O nce you have experienced this picturesque town, you will understand why it draws visitors from all directions. It's a place where neighbours say hello and no one needs to honk. You feel as though you've stepped outside of time — the pace of life is from a bygone era. There are no high-rise buildings, no strip plazas, and no malls; Creemore has a deep kind of quiet peace.

Creemore, in Nottawasaga Township in the County of Simcoe, is situated on the Mad River, on County Road 9, just 24 kilometres (15 miles) southeast of Collingwood. It was Senator J.R. Gowan of Barrie, at the request of a village resident, who selected a name for the village. He suggested Creemore, from the compound Gaelic word *cree mohr*, meaning "big heart." He certainly got the name right. It seems that everyone in Creemore is known by their first name.

The village itself was originally founded in the 1840s. By 1845 two early settlers, Nulty and Webster, formed a partnership and built a lumber mill and a gristmill on the Mad River. This certainly helped to promote settlement, and by 1849 Edward Webster opened the first post office. Webster had already operated a store in the settlement. G.I. Bolster worked as Webster's clerk before eventually opening his own business and becoming the postmaster. Other early pioneer settlers included T. Tupper, J.A. McDonald, the Bowermans, and Sam Wilcox.

It was the water power on the Mad River that attracted industries. The first carding mill in the township was operated at Creemore, and by the 1880s there were three hotels and four churches as well. The population of Creemore, by 1889, was nearing 800 residents. On November 20th of that year, a bylaw was passed to make Creemore a village.

Creemore is quite a magical place in the spring, when area rivers rise and beckon the trout from the bay. Some say the Mad River offers the best trout fishing in this part of Ontario. Summer breezes off the spring-fed hillsides of Creemore keep the residents cool. A walking tour of the community reveals beautiful Victorian architecture and numerous shops featuring antiques, clocks, specialty tea pots, interior decorating, original artwork, trendy clothes, Victorian lingerie, eco-friendly children's wear, hand-carved signs, a butcher, a barber, an excellent bookstore, and even a candlestick maker. There surely must be a baker here, too.

The Hughes homestead near Creemore is well-known to the locals for "unexplained activity." The farmhouse, built circa 1860, has been the scene of many ghostly apparitions. None of the activity has been malicious; in fact, the Hughes family has had farming assistance from what they believe to be their other-worldly predecessors on the farm; some activity seems to relate directly to a native trail running the escarpment ridge. (To read more about the Creemore hauntings, please refer to this writer's book *Haunted Ontario Revisited*).

Today Creemore has become quite famous for its beer — namely, Creemore Springs Brewery Limited. In 1987 John Wiggins established the brewery for three good reasons: the building was already owned by Wiggins, the original investors owned an artesian well in the area, and it seemed to be the natural thing to slake one's thirst.

When John Wiggins opened the front door of Creemore Springs Brewery on August 15, 1987, he sold out of beer in four hours. Not surprising when you hear that world beer guru Michael Jackson (not the singer) calls Creemore Springs Premium Lager the best lager produced in North America.

At Creemore Springs they brew beer the old-fashioned way — pure and simple. They use only clear spring water, the finest malted barley, imported hops from the Czech Republic, and select yeast. The beer is brewed in small batches using an open-fired copper kettle method. In accordance with the Bavarian Purity Law of 1516, they use no additives, no preservatives, no adjuncts, no pasteurization, and no compromise.

In 1991 the company won "gold" for the best lager at the Toronto Beer and Food festival. A year later they won it again. By 1993 Creemore Springs won a *Toronto Star* readers' poll as the best micro-brewed beer in the province. That year, expansion efforts were completed, giving the brewery an annual volume of 1,200,000 litres.

In 1995 Creemore Springs spent another summer in short supply. The company reported that eager consumers were soon learning the secret Creemore delivery routes. And self-appointed investigators indicated that consumers were spotted in the wee hours outside beer stores, waiting in ambush!

A year later the brewery won another prestigious award: the gold medal for Pilsner Lager Category in the World Beer Championships. In November of that year, Creemore Springs released a second beer, UrBock. This seasonal phenomenon took the beer industry by storm. UrBock is now, according to Creemore Springs, "a legend to be appreciated each Christmas."

Creemore Springs Brewery Limited has helped to attract a considerable tourist market to the community. Their store is located on the main street and guided brewery tours are offered. Visitors can treat themselves to a taste test. Clothing with the Creemore label is also for sale in the building.

Some old landmarks surviving in the village today are four churches built in the 1800s; the jail and the Parry house by the river, both of which date back to the 1860s; three hotels and the Casey Block, which once housed a sleigh and carriage shop and a cheese factory that is now a residential block. Local folklore has it that there is more than one ghost to be seen in the surrounding area. More relics from the past, one presumes. So, sometime when you feel like having a little surprise, a pint of prize-winning beer, a Sunday drive, perhaps, or even a good browse in the friendliest bookstore you'll ever see, steer your car to Creemore.

Curve Lake

The territory known as Upper Canada was purchased by the Crown through a number of First Nations surrenders. Certain areas were set aside for continued use of Natives. As the number of European settlers increased, the Native population was increasingly confined to lands known as "Indian Reserves."

The Royal Proclamation of 1763 addressed First Nations' ownership of land and by so doing confirmed that First Nations did indeed hold title to land. This necessitated the purchase of various tracts of land by the government, land that was paid for at the rate of only a few cents an acre.

It was the beginning of massive immigration into Southern Ontario. Within 41 years (1781–1822), all of this land was surrendered to the British Crown; 8.5 million acres were surrendered by the Mississaugas, alone. This was land bordered by the River Thames on the west, Gananoque River to the east, Lake Simcoe to the north, and the Ottawa River to the northeast.

In 1784 an agreement was made with the Mississauga bands for the sale of land east of the Etobicoke River and west of the Trent River for the purpose of British settlement. At the time, the Natives from the Bay of Quinte, the Rice Lake and Lindsay area, the Toronto area, and the Thames district travelled to Carrying Place for the formal exchange of land for gifts and money. Sir John Johnson, superintendent general of Indian Affairs, was present and distributed arms, ammunition, and tobacco to the Native parties.

The lands, as they were negotiated, were known to be bordered by the Tobeka Creek (Etobicoke) on the west and the Crawford Purchase on the east, running from Lake Ontario as far back as Rice Lake; west of Rice Lake, as far back as a day's journey, or more commonly "the distance at which a gunshot can be heard." For this reason it became known as "The Gunshot Treaty." Notably, the Gunshot Treaty was not ratified until the 1923 Williams Treaty, because no payment was ever made for the 1787 cession of parts of the counties of Northumberland, Durham, and York.

During the Toronto Purchase in 1805, Chief Quenepenon bitterly complained to British officials about the treatment of Natives by early settlers. He stated, "The inhabitants (of Toronto) drive us away instead of helping us and we want to know why we are served in that manner. Colonel Butler told us the farmers would help us, but instead of doing so, when we encamp on the shore, they drive us off and shoot our dogs and never give us any assistance as was promised to our chiefs.

"The farmers call us dogs and threaten to shoot us in the same manner when we go on their land. Our dogs, not knowing that they are doing wrong, run after sheep and pigs. When Sir John Johnson came up to purchase the Toronto lands we gave them without hesitation and were told we should always be taken care of and we made no bargain for the land but left it to himself (to determine the price). Now you want another piece of land. We cannot say no. But it is hard for us to give away any more land, the young men and women have found fault with so much having been sold; it is true we are poor and the women say it will be worse if we part with any more."

Despite these misgivings, Quenepenon produced a map of birch bark representing the Burlington Bay tract. He then spoke, "We ask no price, but leave it to the generosity of our Father."

The first missionary groups to begin work with Natives were the New England Company, formed in 1694 in the New England colonies. The New England Company, a non-commercial missionary society, moved to Upper Canada in 1822. Their goal was to work for and help settle the Natives. In 1829 the New England Company received a land grant for 1,600 acres in the north end of Smith Township, Peterborough County. The company's mission was to settle those Natives living in the remote parts of Newcastle District. The Native community of Curve Lake, originally Mud Lake, was born.

The company was also responsible for sending missionaries to Rice, Mud, and Scugog Lakes, Bay of Quinte, and Grand River to establish missions. Since the missionary society was wholly-dependent on private donations, costs were always kept at a minimum.

The property at the Mud Lake settlement was a tax-free grant from the government to the North West Company. Ten to 12 families resided in the Mud Lake vicinity and wished to remain there. The company agent, Reverend Scott, attempted to persuade the group to relocate to Lake Scugog. Scott was well aware of costs and felt one teacher and one preacher would be sufficient — no need to establish yet another community. The Natives at Mud Lake refused to leave the high quality, year-round fishing, the abundant game and fowl, the plentiful sugar maples, the wild rice, and the cranberries.

The Native village of Mud Lake came into being in 1830. Reverend Scott described his goals at this time by stating, "I had the greatest satisfaction of taking the Indians from their scattered wigwams and gave each family a strong and comfortable habitation with a cellar where a good supply of potatoes is laid in for the winter."

Further change was in the offing even after a number of buildings had been erected. Missionaries and government officials felt it would be in the Natives' best interest to move the group to Chemong Lake. There the water was so low that year that a canoe could scarcely be paddled through the lake. If the Natives remained in such a swampy tract, there would be great suffering in the summer months from fever. The next year the situation improved as the water level rose and a dam was built at Buckhorn.

By 1857 the village was growing. Each family had a parcel of land, from one to four acres, and the community numbered 96 individuals. Public property consisted of a log church, a few farm implements, and some stock. The settlement was composed of 17 houses and six barns.

In 1865 Reverend Gilmour recorded a conversation he had had with John Irons, a band member there. Irons protested that although the Mud Lake people had land, it was not really their own, as in actuality it belonged to the New England Company. The Natives were discouraged because they could never call it their own. In 1889 Daniel Whetung wrote, "Our agent calls this place New England Company's Estate not Indian Reserve. He tells us that the company could sell the place." In this case both Irons and Whetung were of the first generation of men educated in the ways of the non-native. They felt the New England Company was harmful to the community as a whole because it held the deed to the land. The people of Mud Lake had merely the status of tenant or lessee. If they did not abide by company bylaws they could be evicted.

The Department of Indian Affairs proposed that the company convey the lands to the Crown in trust, and on June 4, 1898, the land granted to the New England Company in 1837 was transferred to the Dominion Government in trust for the First Nations people. In 1913 the Mud Lake reserve was purchased by the government from the company and the monies came from the Mud Lake annuity. It was ironic that the Natives had to buy back their land in order to have a home, when they once owned and occupied thousands of acres.

Curve Lake Reserve still reveals the signs of the New England Company planning. In 1893 the land was surveyed and sub-divided into lots, with location tickets given to the occupant of each lot. Many of the two-storey frame houses built by the company still remain on these lots. Location tickets for a 50-acre farm lot were given to occupants who had cleared 20 acres for agriculture. Only six of these were ever handed out.

During the depression years, the Curve Lake band council supported relief measures such as lending $5 from the band capital to each individual requesting it. Certain measures were necessary in the 1930s, as cash was scarce when the basket market disappeared, tourism declined, and the price of pelts hit rock bottom. Eventually, the Department of Indian Affairs refused to permit loans from Mud Lake funds. As an alternative the government began a two-month work program to construct a road into the village and paid each worker 20 cents an hour. Although the Natives were poor, no one starved.

In 1966 Clifford and Eleanor Whetung opened a new outlet, called Whetung's Ojibwa Crafts, for crafts in Curve Lake. This heralded a prosperous business in that field and for the area. From the outlet's humble beginnings, the Whetungs have built a business in aboriginal arts and crafts that is now famous across the country. Traditional and contemporary artistic expressions of Canada's First Peoples have been gathered from reserves across the country and housed in an attractive building guarded by huge totem poles at the front entrance. Ritual masks from the Pacific Northwest, pottery of the Mohawks, and baskets of the Mi'kmaq from eastern Canada are among the items for sale. Handsomely, traditionally dressed fur and leather dolls, handcrafted moccasins, clothing, jewellery, and keepsakes are abundant in the building. Paintings and sculptures from a people who have always been known for their unique and beautiful art are found in a gallery equal to any city gallery in its layout, security, and atmospheric controls. Warmed in winter by a huge stone fireplace that reaches five metres (15 feet) to the ceiling, their art gallery houses the work of many well-known Native artists, and it is well-attended year round.

The traditions are also alive and well there. The local band have their Medicine People and use their purification lodges regularly. They are also open to sharing some of their culture with non-natives, which is a gesture truly to be treasured, given their past experiences with non-natives.

Curve Lake is certainly one Indian Reservation that has recovered some of the Native pride that is inherent in Natives — true to nature and a close relationship to this earth. We need to be grateful for the survival of this heritage in a time when our earth is threatened by our unwillingness to accept and celebrate the differences we see in others.

Gore's Landing

The Natives regarded Rice Lake as a very sacred place. It was here they brought their aged chiefs and wounded warriors for purification; it was here the Mississaugas initiated the tradition of burning off the vegetation on the Rice Lake Plains on the southern shore. This practice encouraged the growth of the coarse grass so loved by deer and gave their lake its name — Pemedash-da-kota, meaning Lake of the Burning Plains.

When the Wisconsin glacier receded from southern Ontario 12,000 years ago, meltwater lakes, including the Kawarthas, were formed. Although Rice Lake, located north of Port Hope and Cobourg, is commonly included in the chain of Kawartha lakes, geologically it is separate. Its origin is actually pre-glacial.

Vegetation types arranged themselves in belts parallel to the retreating ice front and shifted northward following the ice. First was a belt of low tundra-like vegetation, followed by northern coniferous forests of white spruce on the uplands and black spruce on the bottomlands, with willow shrubs, birch, and poplars in the meadows.

One large mammal that prefers this vegetation type is the woodland caribou. In the 1980s, the heel bone of one of this species was uncovered by Derek McBride while building an addition to his cottage, near Webbs Bay on the south shore of Rice Lake.

Since European settlement began, in the 1840s, farmers on the Rice Lake Plains and residents of Gore's Landing have discovered arrowheads, stone pipes, skinning knives, pottery shards, and burial

Archives of Ontario

Gore's Landing. Local Ojibwa guide Billy Hogan and his family on an outing on Rice Lake.

sites that testify to the presence of early Natives who lived and hunted on the shores of Rice Lake.

According to lore, a peculiar crevice in a large granite stone at Sager Point, east of Harwood, was used by the Natives to sharpen their tools. It is known locally as a Native rubbing stone.

In 1792 the first lieutenant-governor of Upper Canada, John Graves Simcoe, encouraged loyalists who were still in America to emigrate to Upper Canada. As a result Treaty No. 20 was signed in Port Hope in 1818 by the superintendent-general of Indian Affairs, on behalf of His Majesty, King George III, and by the chiefs of the Mississauga Nations. This treaty opened up 1,951,000 acres in the northern sections of the Newcastle District. For this surrender of land, the Nations of the Kawarthas were guaranteed an annual payment of 740 pounds.

In 1973, a trading post was established at the mouth of the Otanabee River on the north shore of Rice Lake. By the last quarter of the 18th century, almost all the important furs were "trapped-out" (depleted by over-trapping) along the north shore of Lake Ontario. In the early 1800s wild rice became an important trade item for the Rice Lake Natives. In 1817 it was reported that the rice of this lake grew so thickly that up to 10,000 bushels a year were available for harvesting. Sadly, the wild rice beds have disappeared due to a number of factors, including the change in lake levels following the construction of dams for the Trent Canal. The creation of the Trent system raised water levels on many lakes. In July 1928, a hurricane wreaked further havoc and, since 1950, the introduction of bottom-feeding carp has destroyed most of the roots of the remaining rice plants.

In the 1840s, a settlement started on the south shore of the lake. The settlers called their home Gore's Landing, named after Thomas S. Gore, a British Navy captain who had owned land here in 1845. This was not the first visit here by white people. In 1825 Peter Robinson brought 1,875 Irish settlers from Cobourg to Gore's Landing, across Rice Lake, and up the Otanabee River to settle in Peterborough.

Gore's Landing began to prosper when it became the terminal point of the plank road from Cobourg to Rice Lake in 1847. A stagecoach connection offered residents and visitors the opportunity to travel. A private boarding school, F.W. Barron Boys' School, was opened by a former headmaster of Upper Canada College. A hotel, a tavern, a general store, and several small industries made up the business section. In the early 1900s, Gore's Landing became a boatbuilding centre and a port of call for Rice Lake steamers. More than one regatta was held at Gore's Landing.

Gore's Landing also has its fair share of famous people who resided here at one time or another, such as the famous nature poet Archibald Lampman; Derwyn T. Owen, who became Anglican Primate of All Canada; and J.D. Kelly, an historical artist.

Few Canadians are aware of a famous artist who built his summer home on the shore of Rice Lake, in Gore's Landing. On January 20, 1845, one of Canada's most prolific but least-known painters, Gerald Sinclair Hayward, was born. A man of many talents, Hayward dared to pursue life to the fullest. He enlisted for frontier service with the Port Hope Infantry Company in November, 1865. He was awarded a Queen's Medal and discharged in April, 1866, with the rank of ensign. Next, he tried farming and railroading, but neither seemed to satisfy him. He was in his early twenties when he decided to start an entirely new career.

The art of painting miniature portraits and scenes appealed to Hayward, but it was not widely practiced in Canada, so he went to study at the Royal Academy schools in London, England, in 1870. While there, he was commissioned by many members of the English, German, and Russian courts to do miniature portraits on ivory. He painted Queen Victoria, the Prince of Wales (later King Edward VII), Princess Alice, the Countess of Minto, the Duke and Duchess of Buckingham, Lord and Lady Caven, the Empress of Prussia, and the Czarina of Russia. Later, in Canada, he painted the prime ministers MacDonald and Laurier.

Hayward gave his first exhibition, of 90 modern miniatures, in the United States at the Avery Galleries in New York in 1889 and continued to exhibit throughout the country. One leading newspaper said, "Mr. Hayward has become world-famous in his exclusive field and has painted more than a thousand distinguished persons in America on coming out from London." Another paper wrote, "His work is strongly individualistic — the eye full of life, hair freely treated, fidelity in tint of complexion, with perfect harmony in tone of background, combine to make the living portrait possible to obtain."

Hayward took up residence in New York City, but returned to Canada to build a summer home in Gore's Landing on Rice Lake in 1900. He had never really strayed too far from his birthplace, Port Hope. Hayward built a magnificent villa with screened verandas overlooking the lake. He named his home The Willows. This was his favourite retreat, and he was so enchanted with the panoramic view from his tower window that he later painted the lake and its many islands on the walls of his dining room.

As church warden he assisted in the building of St. George's Anglican Church in the village, and much of its artistic appearance is due to his interest in the construction. When he died in New York on March 31, 1926, his ashes were brought to Gore's Landing by his daughter and buried in the cemetery of the church. The *Toronto Star Weekly* published an article on Hayward on April 3 of that year, stating, "In the passing of Gerald Sinclair Hayward, world-famous miniature painter, Canada loses one of her greatest artists."

Unfortunately, he has been all but forgotten as a Canadian artist. The murals of Rice Lake on his dining room walls are covered with coats of paint, and his beautiful home, The Willows, is now the Victoria Inn. Gerald Sinclair Hayward's tower room is a special one; I have stayed there myself, with my wife.

The Natives went to Rice Lake for purification and that was our experience, too. It was a wild night of rain and lightning; you could open windows in three of the four directions (and we did). The power of nature there was something to behold; we felt blessed to share that space and were amazingly refreshed by the storm. The lake was always sacred to the Natives, and Hayward's home was sacred to him. When that's the case, the feeling is always there for others to share.

You really should pay Gore's Landing a visit. There are a number of architectural delights there that were built between 1848 and 1895. It is obvious that, in their incredible and unique beauty, these buildings were special to their owners. It's a joy to look at and touch what was another's sacred space.

Holland Landing

To his neighbours, Samuel Lount was an amiable chap. He was outspoken and campaigned for his beliefs. Samuel left Pennsylvania in 1811 and arrived near Holland Landing, where he worked hard and prospered as a farmer, a blacksmith, and a surveyor. He won a position as a Reformer and member of the legislative assembly for Simcoe County. On December 7, 1837, his life looked pretty grim. In the days leading up to this date, he became involved in William Lyon Mackenzie's uprising against the government, the Family Compact. On that fateful day of action, he was in joint command of the rebel forces who met at Montgomery's Tavern (which was located just north of Yonge and Eglinton). Shortly after the rebels' defeat, he became a fugitive of the law and attempted to flee the country.

William Lyon Mackenzie escaped and remained in exile for several years before he was able to return to Canada. Unfortunately for Samuel, he was captured before he reached the American border. Samuel was convicted of high treason by the government on April 12, 1838; he was escorted to the gallows and hanged. Such was the fate of Holland Landing's spokesman.

The village of Holland Landing had only been surveyed in 1811. Located near the site of a sawmill built by John Eves in 1808 and on the east branch of the Holland River, it was a perfect spot for settlement and industry. It was also only 48 kilometres (30 miles) north of York (known today as Toronto). The Natives had used this very spot as a landing place because it marked the end of the portage from Lake Simcoe and what is now called Georgian Bay. Archaeological evidence revealed the existence of a one-time Native village and burial ground. Many villages established in Ontario at the same time as Holland Landing were located on former Native village sites.

Quakers, Mennonites, and United Empire Loyalists arrived to settle the town. The residents of this newly established community first called it St. Albans and later Beverly. By 1821 Peter Robinson established Red Mills, which quickly became the most important mill in the area. Robinson even shipped the flour he made to Europe. That same year, a post office was opened and the citizens renamed their village Holland Landing, after Major Samuel Holland, surveyor-general of the Province of Quebec in the late 18th century.

The community seemed destined for greatness. By 1825 a stage service ran daily from York, and by 1833 a steamboat connection had been set up. All of this encouraged further growth and led to the establishment of several industries. Among them were a brewery, a distillery, two tanneries, a foundry, and Ellerby's carding and fulling mill. In 1851 the plank road was completed and this facilitated a growing wheat and livestock trade. Cargo ships on the Holland River made Holland Landing a major shipping depot between Lake Simcoe and York.

The completion of the Northern Railway in 1853 altered the booming commerce of the village. People began to travel less by road and water, and the need for such a shipping point diminished. In the late 19th century the owner of the Toby Mill relocated his business to Collingwood, after a dispute with the village over taxes, and area businesses that were dependent on the mill suffered as a result. A number of disastrous fires swept through and demolished most of the remaining businesses, and by 1921 the village population had decreased significantly.

The village of Holland Landing is located adjacent to the market-gardening area known as the Holland Flats. Originally, this area was settled by many Dutch immigrants who were familiar with land management. They were willing and able to turn a marsh into a productive and vital piece of land. The Dutch settlers had drained the land in their home country (with dykes and ditches) and used that same expertise here. The village of Ansnorveldt was established, along with productive gardens near Holland Landing.

A major catastrophe struck the Holland Flats in October 1954, when Hurricane Hazel swept southern Ontario. The Holland Flats literally disappeared under six to nine metres (20 to 30 feet) of water. The village of Ansnorveldt was submerged, homes were swept away or overturned and the losses totalled in the millions. After the water had retreated, the residents attempted to remove the remaining water with large pumping systems. The situation was overwhelming; the damage seemed irreparable. Nevertheless, with the aid of county, provincial, and federal funds, work was started to restore the land, and within the year, Holland Flats was once again fully productive.

The agricultural production of Holland Flats is crucial for the province of Ontario. As urban, commercial, and industrial development in the southern parts of the province swallow the remaining market garden areas, this is both obvious and significant. Perhaps Samuel Lount was a model area resident. He was willing to fight for the things he believed in. This is the kind of resolve needed to protect this agricultural mecca for the future.

Ivanhoe

Ivanhoe, like many of Central Ontario's smaller communities, has taken immense pride in preserving its distinctive quality of life for more than 150 years. This tiny hamlet has kept a firm hold on the basics of life, a hold which some larger towns and cities have relinquished. The Ivanhoe Cheese Company is the major centre of employment here and has some responsibility for the community functioning much like a family.

The first record of land settlement at Ivanhoe, situated on Highway 62 between Madoc and Belleville, was in 1803. These early settlers of Ivanhoe and the township were of Irish, Scottish, and English descent, with names such as Ketcheson, Ostrom, Denike, Luke, Foster, and Ashley. Later families arrived with the names of Ray, Ryrett, McKee, Shaw, Rollins, Emo, Stout, Gunning, Ranson, Carscallen, MacMillan, and Gauen from Ireland; Harvey, Wood, Fleming, Roy, McMullen, and Archibald from Scotland; Tummon, Chapman, King, Lidster, and Prest from England; and United Empire Loyalists such as Reid and Mitz.

To get to Madoc in the early years of settlement, Ivanhoe dwellers used a raft to cross Moira Lake, then known as Hog Lake (Hog Lake got its name from a rock that resembled a hog's back). Sometime later Bronson's Bridge was built.

The first post office in Ivanhoe was established on July 1, 1850, and was named St. George. This name was changed to the Ivanhoe Post Office on April 1, 1857, at the suggestion of an Irish schoolteacher by the name of Thomas Emo. He had been reading Sir Walter Scott's novel of the same name. Since the fictional hero characterized the Irish spirit, he promptly named the post office after the rugged-but-compassionate medieval warrior.

Even in the early days, Ivanhoe's main and thriving business was cheese. In 1870 a two-storey building was constructed on the property of George Rollins, on the 7th Concession of Huntingdon Township, for the purpose of making cheese. The structure consisted of a cooking room on the first floor and a curing room on the second. The milk came in at the curing-room level, where it was conducted by a pipe to vats on the lower floor. Because the curing room was upstairs, it was necessary for large and heavy loads of cheese to be carried downstairs. The factory was called the Ivanhoe Cheese Factory, and its first president was Henry Gauen. He established himself in Ivanhoe on a land grant, which he received for his service in one of the expedition parties that searched in the Arctic for Sir John Franklin.

In the early days of the cheese company, workers collected milk cans from local farms twice a day. The company furnished the milk wagons as well as the cans. When the wagons became worn, the company did not replace them. Each dairy farmer who drew milk was, from then on, held responsible for supplying his own wagon and his own cans.

On December 28, 1889, seven men appeared in the law office of A.F. Wood in Madoc, to request the incorporation of The Beulah Cheese and Butter Co-operative. This was done on the advice of cheese buyers in Belleville who felt that the name Ivanhoe should be dropped because it had a reputation for inferior quality products. It was also decided that the quality should improve. British importers were refusing any further cheese associated with the name "Ivanhoe."

In the same period of time, a second factory was under construction on the property of James Gunning, at the bottom of the hill on the 7th Concession. Beulah Cheese was thought to be better quality and, consequently, could be priced higher. John Fleming was one of many who worked for both companies. He served as the factory salesman from 1895 until his sudden death in 1913.

In 1926 yet another new Beulah factory was erected on a site at the four corners. Upon its completion the old factory was torn down and the lumber was used to build the cheesemaker's home. Business flourished and additions were made to the curing room. In 1965 a dairy bar was opened that was so popular it was enlarged twice.

The Beulah factory continued to produce Ivanhoe's fine cheese until February 1, 1978, when the building was destroyed by fire. Immediate arrangements and plans for a new factory were begun. In April 1979 the new Beulah Co-op Cheese Company was officially opened by the Honourable William Newman, minister of agriculture and food for Ontario. In the early part of 1983, the factory once again took on the original name: The Ivanhoe Cheese Company Ltd.

Today the Ivanhoe Cheese Company is a thriving business and remains an important partner in the community. It is a living historical link to Ivanhoe's past. Its cheddar and specialty cheeses can be found in grocery stores province-wide and are also favoured by American tourists. Their extra-old white cheddar is superb, and their unique horseradish cheddar is relished for its bite.

Not only did Ivanhoe and its cheese company produce quality cheese, it also had some unique citizens. Henry Gauen, the first president of the Ivanhoe Cheese Company and an Arctic explorer, was one of them.

In 1845 Sir John Franklin attempted to find the Northwest Passage in order to chart a navigable route to the riches of China and East India. For 300 years prior to Franklin's expedition, explorers had searched in vain for this route. Exploration caught the fancy of dreamers. Franklin was well aware of the mysteries of the north, the maze of land and sea, the crushing power of ice, the cold, the darkness, and the loneliness. Scattered clusters of bones attest to the frosty plight of many a good sailor.

Franklin, with his two ships, the *Erebus* and the *Terror*, set sail from the Thames on the morning of May 19, 1845, carrying 134 officers and men. The last sighting of Franklin and his ships was in July of the same year when, in Baffin Bay, they met two whaling ships. Franklin's ships were waiting for the right conditions in order to cross Baffin Bay to Lancaster Sound. There was no concern about Franklin's whereabouts until 1847, when there had still been no communication. The British Admiralty in London sent out three expeditions that year to relieve Franklin. Captain Henry Kellett was directed to sail to the Bering Strait, while a second expedition under the command of James Clark Ross was ordered to sail to Lancaster Sound. The third expedition, led by Dr. John Rae and Sir John Richardson, went down the Mackenzie River. The failure of all three expeditions to find any trace of Franklin sparked some urgency concerning the crews of both ships.

On April 4, 1850, the *Toronto Globe* ran an advertisement announcing "A 20,000 pound reward to be given by Her Majesty's Government to any party or parties, of any country, who shall render efficient assistance to the crews of the discovery ships under the command of Sir John Franklin."

Henry Gauen was part of the voyage in search of Franklin that headed out from Plymouth, England, on January 20, 1850, with two ships named the *Enterprise* and the *Investigator*. Gauen served as the ship's carpenter and was under the command of Captain McClure.

McClure's ship, the *Investigator*, was separated from its consort and arrived at the Bering Strait on July 29, 1850. By September 9th he was 96 kilometres (60 miles) from the western stretch of Viscount Melville Sound. On September 26 the *Investigator* was sealed in, surrounded by thick sheets of ice.

On October 10th of that year, McClure turned his attention to other matters — not to finding Franklin, but rather to discovering the Northwest Passage. His lookout had spotted open water in the distance, and he wondered if it was a continuation of Barrow Strait. McClure led a sled party across the ice to the land on the east side of the channel. He and the small party climbed up a 500-metre (1,500 feet) rise and from that vantage point saw the ice-packed channel. Dr. Armstrong, medical attendant to the crew, was convinced that the highway to England from ocean to ocean lay before them, but McClure needed to set foot on shore of the passage himself.

Eleven days later McClure and a party set out again on an exhausting five-day journey along the eastern shore of Banks Island to the end of the channel. On October 26, 1850, Robert McClure, standing on a 200-metre (600 foot) promontory, confirmed the presence of a water route from Atlantic to Pacific. The Northwest Passage had been discovered. McClure and crew were eligible for the prize of 10,000 pounds that had been promised by the English government for the discovery.

Regardless of his success, McClure remained to search for Franklin. By September 9, 1852, the crew were down to one meal a day. In October, a delegation pleaded with the captain for an increase in food, but McClure refused. It was reported that Sub-Lieutenant Robert Wynniatt went mad. Each man weighed about 15 kilograms (35 pounds) less than when they had left England, and 20 were ill with scurvy.

A few years ago, the people of Ivanhoe cleared the grave site of Henry Gauen, erected a fence, and placed a tombstone there in his honour.

During one outing Henry Gauen was attacked by a polar bear. Henry kept the bear at bay until he managed to shoot it with his gun, but carried scars from the bear's claws on his back for the rest of his life. Notwithstanding a polar bear attack, Henry actually put on his skates and was, quite possibly, the first man to ever skate on Artic ice.

The winter of 1852–53 dragged on, and the health of the crew declined further; two crew members went insane and howled all night. By the end of January, a clerk, Joseph Paine, and one of the mates, John Boyle, had died of scurvy. A day later Lieutenant Pim of the *Resolute* found the *Investigator*. On April 15th the remaining crew of the *Investigator* set off by sled for two vessels moored off Melville Island. It was a ghastly journey — half the men were lame from scurvy, unable to stand, shrunken, hollow-eyed, and slightly crazed.

By the September 25, 1854, Gauen and what others remained of the *Investigator's* crew had arrived home in England. They were presented with 10,000 pounds, 80 pounds of which was Gauen's share. He was also presented with a silver medal embossed with a sailing ship, specially cast for Arctic explorers. He subsequently married an English woman and came to live in the hamlet of Ivanhoe.

As for Franklin, it was later discovered that he and his two crews had indeed perished over a period of time. Several factors contributed to this loss of life, one being the harsh environment. Another factor leading to the death of some crew members was discovered to be lead poisoning. It has been calculated that each crew member would have been allotted about .25 kilograms (.5 pounds) of tinned food every second day — a regular ingestion of lead from the lead-tin solder used to seal the tins. Furthermore, it was later found that the side seams on some of the tins were incomplete and the food had spoiled, a recipe for botulism. Exact details will remain a secret, lost to history.

Mr. Henry Gauen died in July 1889 at the age of 77. He was buried just north of Ivanhoe, on the west side of the road, on the land that he had settled. Over the years his gravesite became overgrown and lost from view. However, the people of Ivanhoe have since cleared the grave site, erected a fence, and placed a tombstone in his honour, just one example of their pride in the community.

The citizens of Ivanhoe have chosen to remember and be grateful to the man who helped establish a cheese company for the community, and I am grateful to them. Henry Gauen was my great-great grandfather.

Kapuskasing

The majority of folks say Ka'puskasing
But if we had a chat
They'd say Kapuss'kasing'
And say it, just like that
And if they went to live and sing
They'd soon be saying Kap!
So I guess it doesn't matter much
But I like Kapuss'kasing'
This Native place by the river's bend
Needs a different ring!

— Allanah Douglas

The region that we know as Kapuskasing today was primarily used by fur traders. The Hudson's Bay Company and the Old Northwest Traders both set up operations in the area. In the early 1900s, the National Transcontinental Railway (now CN) pushed through this wilderness and a station was built where the railway crossed the river. It was first known as McPherson and was in 1917 changed to Kapuskasing, a Cree word meaning "the place where the river bends."

Back in 1914, the Canadian government decided to purchase 1,280 acres of land west of the Kapuskasing River and south of the Transcontinental Railway tracks. Their objective was to establish an experimental farm. They chose this area because it was part of the fertile Great Clay Belt region of Northern Ontario. Scientists believed they

Archives of Ontario

Kapuskasing circa 1914. First built as a prisoner of war camp and subsequently used to house potential war veterans in an attempt to settle the area.

could develop hardier varieties of crops that would be able to withstand the harsh climate of the north.

The station was, however, converted that same year into an internment camp for illegal immigrants and prisoners of war. These internees built a barracks, hospital, canteen, YMCA, post office, bakery, and a supply depot. They also managed to clear 100 acres of land that first year. By the end of 1915, the camp had 1,200 internees and 250 soldiers to supervise and operate the complex. Incredible as it may sound, these internees had cleared another 500 acres of land by the end of that year. By 1917 most of the internees had been paroled due to labour shortages, and 400 prisoners of war replaced them. The camp remained open until 1920, when the last prisoner of war was repatriated. Thirty-two German prisoners died while at the camp and were buried across from the present-day public cemetery.

The Canadian government then embarked on a new land settlement scheme for returned soldiers. Government officials managed to route

101 settlers to Kapuskasing. Each soldier was assigned a 100-acre lot. A training school for these new pioneers was built at Monteith and dormitories were built to provide housing until the settlers could erect their own homes. The government also provided farm implements, stock, and seed at very low cost to the settlers.

Determined to make this work, the government built a sawmill, a planing mill, a blacksmith shop, a steam laundry, a store, and a school on the east bank of the Kapuskasing River. The settlers were subsequently organized into groups, and each party was supervised by a government foreman. The goal was to clear the land for farming.

It wasn't long before these settlers had had enough. They felt like little more than work gangs, there to satisfy some government idea of settling the north. Just back from fighting a war, this scheme seemed as much like a POW camp as it did a place to get a fresh start. It was all about control. The men were unhappy with the arrangements and the majority of them abandoned the entire project. Out of 101 settlers, nine remained. They were Mair, McCall, Yorke, Wing, MacMinn, Grant, Le Marrier, Gough, and Poolton.

Things began to look up for Kapuskasing in 1922, when the Spruce Falls Power and Paper Company built a pulp and paper mill. Several years later a newsprint mill was constructed to produce paper for the *New York Times*. Both mills received their power from a new hydro development 80 kilometres (50 miles) to the north.

It was the mill workers and the original settlers of 1920 that really put Kapuskasing on the map. They planned their business section as a circle, with five streets radiating outward. Still influenced heavily by their government-sponsored origins, they named the streets after the premier of Ontario (E.C. Drury) and his members of cabinet.

Kapuskasing was incorporated in 1921, with the motto *Oppidum ex Silvis* meaning "Town out of the Forest."

A new paper mill with a daily capacity of 64 tonnes of cellulose started production in 1945 at the Spruce Falls company site.

Yes, this town beside the river's bend that sprung from forests cleared
Was carved out, in the northland by folks that had no fear.
They did not fear the cold or snow, or the government's heavy hand

nor the work they had to do there, to claim this rugged land.
And so their lives keep going, even as I bring, this story of the
people, of sweet, Kapuss'kasing.

— Allanah Douglas

Keene

Have you ever travelled somewhere and suddenly felt you were in the presence of something sacred, something special, and had some sense of having been there before?

This indeed was my experience when, about 20 years ago, I ventured to the community of Keene. Somehow I found myself in a place that challenged my memory. Why was it so familiar? What was I sensing? This is my story. I ventured out that day to visit Keene and the sacred burial mounds, and to learn the history.

Keene itself is located on the banks of the Indian River, just before it flows into Rice Lake. The countryside, made up of rolling hills, was at one time heavily wooded. The sparkling waters and the islands of Rice Lake create a perfect picture-postcard. It is truly a place of divine creation. It was here the Natives lived, hunted, fought, and died long before Thomas and Andres Carr arrived in 1820. Their presence was but a mere dot on the timeline of this rolling land. John Gilchrist, the first doctor in Ontario to be granted a licence to practice "Physic Surgery and Midwifery," has been credited with the initial development of the community.

The good doctor was quite an entrepreneur. He built a gristmill and a sawmill on the Indian River, not to mention a distillery and houses for the workmen. In a short time, he became a lumber baron and ran a flourishing export business. By 1850, Keene's population had risen to 400 people.

Water transportation played a key role in the early development of this community. In 1882, however, the mainline of the Canadian Northern Railway from Toronto to Belleville was laid down about 2 kilometres (1.5

David Boyle, the teacher and archeologist, was ultimately responsible for the discovery and preservation of Serpent Mounds at Keene.

miles) north of Keene, and the importance of water transport declined. Keene's industries declined as well.

There was, nevertheless, always something of greater importance located in the landscape near Keene that had somehow gone unnoticed. It was a sacred place to those who knew of such things; it was a site near water, a site where a marvelous grove of oak trees grew. What was it? Why had such a special place been abandoned, neglected, and ignored by those around it? Who changed all of that? David Boyle!

David Boyle was a gifted man of great insight and intuition. He was born the son of a blacksmith in Greenock, Scotland, on May 1, 1842, and immigrated to Ontario in 1856. When Boyle was only 14, he apprenticed to a blacksmith in Eden Mills, Wellington County, Ontario. He was a self-taught individual who rejected the materialistic values of the day. He pursued instead the ideal of self-culture and acquired and imparted knowledge to any who would listen. This quest for knowledge took him to the classroom. During this career his caring and patience led him to teach a deaf-mute girl how to read and write. This was a great accomplishment and amazed many people at the time. Boyle then followed a brief career as a textbook promoter and proprietor of Ye Olde Booke Shoppe and Natural Science Exchange in Toronto. His next career was the field of archaeology.

His first major archaeological excavation began on October 5, 1885, when he investigated the historic Neutral Dwyer ossuaries northwest of Hamilton. He obtained enough artifacts to establish an exhibit in the front window of his bookstore. Boyle dearly wanted to educate people about the importance of the preservation of history. In his opinion enough damage had already been done by early settlers who had desecrated Native gravesites and spread ancient earthen walls over their newly-developed fields. Numerous artifacts were discovered and discarded or destroyed during the 17th and 18th centuries in Ontario. Few people recognized the historic value or the sacredness of such sites (skeletons stored in museums, as well as sacred objects, such as medicine bundles and masks, are being returned to Natives today).

In 1884, Boyle became the curator-archaeologist of the Canadian Institute Museum (1884–1896) and later the Ontario Provincial Museum (1896–1911). It was Boyle who, in 1887, established the Annual Archaeological Reports for Ontario. This was the first periodical published in Canada that was devoted primarily to archaeology. He continued this work until 1908.

During the first week of September 1896, Boyle ventured forth into the field for what was about to become the most thrilling four weeks of discovery in Keene — The Serpent Mounds.

On his arrival, Boyle sought out the property owned by his friend H.T. Strickland of Peterborough. There, on the crest of a hill near the mouth of the Indian River, Boyle first observed the mounds and quickly noted evidence of early relic hunters. Stepping back a distance, he walked to a ridge about 15 metres (50 feet) to the west. It occurred to him, at that point, that the end of the embankment was tapered. He hastened to the other extremity of the structure and saw how it rose abruptly to a height of 1.3 metres (four feet). He knew it right there and then. What he was looking at was a great "serpent mound" like the one discovered in Adam County, Ohio. Boyle walked back and forth, keenly assessing the mound from every direction. No matter what his vantage point, he could still see the head of a serpent at the eastern end of the mound, a tapering tail to the west, and three well-marked convolutions. Boyle measured the structure and realized that each zig-zag section was roughly 13 metres (40 feet) long. He knew the builders intended the structure to be serpentine. The position of the oval mound, accurately in line with the head and neck portion of the long structure, suggested "the ancient combination of serpent and egg." There, in front of him, was a burial effigy mound, and it is still the only example of its kind in Ontario.

Boyle dug in, starting with the oval mound at the eastern extremity of the structure. Soon a trench two metres (six feet) wide, across the mound and to the western end, was completed. He discovered two skeletons in a sitting position, a skull, and long bones at a depth of 0.6 metres (two feet). He concluded that these were recent burials. At a level of one metre (three feet) in the second trench, he located another skeleton lying on its right side and surmised that the body had been placed there prior to the construction of the mound itself. He also found a human skull, an animal mandible, canine teeth, mussel shells, and charcoal. It was near the centre of the mound that he unearthed burnt human bones (not associated with ashes or charcoal), several pottery fragments and, at the base level, a circle of stones "crudely put together" about 1 metre (3 feet) in diameter. Next was the opening of the serpentine structure in two places. The first opening was made about 21 metres (68 feet) from the tail and the second at the eastern extremity, near the head. There he discovered a much-decayed human bone in the first cut and comparatively recent burials less than 45 centimetres (18 inches) from the surface, near the head of the serpent. Boyle also found human remains in the other four elliptical mounds lying along the south side of the serpent.

Boyle began, almost at once, to pressure the government to preserve the site as a provincial park, as an ancient historic site, and as a Native burial ground. He even approached the owner of the property, who offered to sell the four-acre site for $450. The government, unfortunately, had no intention of providing more parks for the public so soon after the creation of Algonquin Park in 1893. It was fortunate, indeed, that the mounds were protected by the owners. In 1933, the Hiawatha band of the Mississauga Nation purchased the property and leased it to the Ontario Department of Lands and Forests. In 1956, the site was turned into a provincial park — 60 years after Boyle had first proposed the idea.

News of the discovery prompted people throughout the county to provide information about other possible mounds and village sites in the area. Soon, Boyle was back to do a field survey of the Rice Lake–Trent River shoreline and islands. At the mouth of the Otonabee River, he found three burial mounds. It was there that he discovered a large engraved stone, resembling a turtle, the back of which was crudely ornamented with concentric circles, scrolls, and shallow depressions or borings. Burial mounds were also discovered on some of islands of Rice Lake. One site revealed a half-seated skeleton with its legs drawn up and its hands on its breast. Around the neck was an eight-strand necklace of copper beads and shell disks, and near the right arm was a perfect tablet, a biconcave gorget, or armour plate, of translucent Mexican onyx.

Boyle believed he had discovered structures that had been made by Middle Point Peninsula people who were indigenous to the Trent water system and who had in some way been influenced by the Ohio Hopewell Indians.

There is a recorded oral account by Paudash, son of Paudash, son of Cheneebeesh, son of Gemoghpenassess. It states, "I, Robert Paudash, with my son Johnson Paudash, am desirous of putting on record for the first time the solemn traditions of the Mississaugas with respect to their present place of settlement in Ontario, and the migration which led them thither. No word of what I am about to say has come from reading, or in any other way than from the mouth of Paudash, my father, who died, aged 75 in the year 1893, the last hereditary chief of the tribe of Mississaugas, situated at Rice Lake, and from the mouth of Cheneebeesh, my grandfather, who died in 1869, at the age of 104, the last sachem, or head chief, of all the Mississaugas [Ojibwa]."

The story refers to the migration of the Ojibwa into southern Ontario around 1690 and what happened in the Rice Lake district. According to Robert Paudash, the Mississaugas held a great council of war and decided to attack the Mohawks and drive them out of what is now southern Ontario. The Mohawks, a fierce and warlike nation, resisted. The Mississaugas travelled down the Severn River to Shunyung (Lake Simcoe) and stopped at Machickning (which means Fish Fence) in the narrows between Lake Simcoe and Lake Couchiching to get supplies of food. There they also received reinforcements, made preparations for a campaign, and divided into two parties. The main body proceeded along the portage, now called Portage Road, to Balsam Lake, while the other party went south to what is now Toronto. After a number of skirmishes, the Mohawks retreated down the valley of the Otanabee and onto Rice Lake. Several battles were fought until they made a stand at what is now Keene.

Robert Paudash adds, "There was a Mohawk village in front of the former site which is a mound in the shape of a serpent, and having four small mounds about its head and body in the form of turtles. These mounds are a pictorial representation of Mohawk totems placed there by the Mississaugas in memory of the occurrence and of the Mohawks. It has been supposed by some to mean more than this, but my father has so stated it.

"The Mohawks fought well, but the Mississaugas were just as good. An attack having been made upon this village the Mohawks were compelled once more to retreat."

Back now, to my personal story.

When I first approached Serpent Mounds, I had a feeling that I had been there before. Climbing up the path, I came to an historic plaque and read the inscription. When I saw the name David Boyle, I knew there had to be a connection. I approached the mounds and then caught sight of the oak trees. I knew immediately that these trees somehow played a significant role in this site, as did the view of Rice Lake. You could sense the sacredness. No words needed to be spoken. Serpent Mounds left me with an impression of beauty, reverence, and mystery.

Serpent Mounds inspired me to learn more about David Boyle and the oak trees. On a trip south, I stopped at a burial mound in the state of Michigan. I needed to compare it to the mound at Keene. Sure enough, the mounds were located in a grove of oaks and were also close to water. The sites looked and felt the same. Coincidences?

If you visit Serpent Mounds, or Keene, or perhaps another place to which you find yourself drawn, don't ignore your feelings. Explore them and you may unlock some mysteries of your own.

Kingston

Exploring the north shore of Lake Ontario in 1671, Sieur de la Salle recommended the building of a fort and fur-trading post at the present site of Kingston. The Natives called this location Cataraqui, meaning "rocks standing in water." On July 12, 1673, Count Frontenac, governor of New France, arrived with a flotilla at Cataraqui and met the local Native chiefs, assuring them of his peaceful intentions. Frontenac then proceeded to construct a fort. The next year, La Salle was appointed commandant of the fort and the beginning of a settlement took place.

When La Salle was away on one of his expeditions, the fort was taken over by Governor de La Barre, Frontenac's successor. The next governor, the Marquis de Denonville, imprisoned two Native chiefs and, in reprisal, the Natives of the district burned the settlers' homes and crops. They besieged the fort for two months. In 1689, Denonville ordered the destruction of the fort and moved the garrison to Montreal. When Count Frontenac again became governor, the fort at Cataraqui was restored. In 1756, the fort was used as a base by French commander-in-chief Montcalm during a battle of the Seven Years' War, fought between the British and the French for the control of what is now Canada. During the war, 1,600 British prisoners were housed at the fort after the French victory of Oswego. One prisoner, by the name of Michael Grass, survived this ordeal to become one of the founders of Kingston. The British captured the fort in 1758, destroyed the fortification, and moved the garrison to Montreal.

For the next 25 years, the area remained deserted. On nearby Carleton Island, a fort was built and many United Empire Loyalists sought refuge here during the American Revolution. Meanwhile, in 1783, Major John Ross had restored the old fort at Cataraqui and became the first commandant of the Imperial Garrison. The fort was renamed Tete-de-Pont Barracks. Surveyor John Collins arrived at the same time and laid out the original town plot of Kingston. When Carleton Island became part of the United States, by the Treaty of Paris, many of the Loyalists moved to the fort at Cataraqui.

Captain Michael Grass arrived in June 1784, with the first group of Loyalists, who lived temporarily in the fort. By October the settlers had built their first homes.

Kingston was originally named King's Town by the United Empire Loyalists who settled there. By the early 1790s, the community boasted 50 homes and stores, including the government store at the lower end of Store Street (now Princess Street). The government established a naval dockyard on Point Frederick, on a site now occupied by the Royal Military College. The marines and shipyard workers at this site were connected by ferry to Kingston. In 1792, Kingston became the seat of government of Upper Canada. The first Executive Council met here on July 17 under Lieutenant-Governor John Graves Simcoe. However, Simcoe did not feel Kingston was a suitable capital and soon moved the government to Newark (Niagara-on-the-Lake) and later York (Toronto).

The geographical location of Kingston, at the mouth of the St. Lawrence, meant that goods were transferred here from river boats to lake boats; this made it a major trading centre between Montreal and the Lakehead. By 1800 Kingston was a regular customs port for American goods.

Kingston was one of the few settlements in Upper Canada where marriage licences were issued. The community, as a result, became known as something of a honeymoon resort.

During the War of 1812, five wooden blockhouses were constructed around the settlement, and the first Fort Henry was built. Although Kingston was never assaulted by American troops during the war, the community did experience some prosperity as a result of troops, sailors, and shipbuilding activities in the vicinity. By then the population had increased to 2,250.

In 1828, a serious bout of typhus broke out among the Irish families brought here during the construction of the Cataraqui Bridge and the Rideau Canal. A cholera plague in 1832 killed 10 percent of the population of Kingston. In 1847 thousands of poor Irish people, who had left Ireland as a result of a potato famine, brought a cholera epidemic to Upper Canada. It was estimated that 1,200 people died from this epidemic in Kingston; they were buried in a mass grave near the Kingston General Hospital.

Kingston was incorporated as a town in 1818. By 1841 the town had become the capital of United Canada, the newly united Upper and Lower Canada. Three years later the government abandoned Kingston as the capital of the province in favour of Montreal. It was during this period that Queen's University was founded.

Many immigrants who arrived in Kingston had no means to proceed any farther and joined the ranks of the unemployed. Begging, gambling, prostitution, and theft became the livelihood of many living on the fringes of Kingston society, as well as the fringes of the town.

The cholera epidemic of 1847 left many widows, orphans, elderly, and disabled persons unable to survive on their own. Kingston officials called a meeting in November of that year to establish a House of Industry (hostel). In December the House of Industry opened its doors and in the first month of operation admitted 183 persons; 175 of them were Irish-born. Of the inmates, 44 were widows (and another three originally listed as widows appear to have married before leaving the hostel), and 63 were children under the age of 10. There were some strange methods used to aid the poor. The guiding principle for charity pertained only to the "deserving poor." Some believed that the poor had brought their misfortunes upon themselves as a result of sloth, dissipation, or other moral lapses. Therefore, the House of Industry had rules. The rules stipulated that no person of bad character, "especially unchaste women with bastard children," should be admitted; the possession or consumption of liquor meant instant eviction.

One of the great social problems among the poor, unsurprisingly, was drunkenness. In 1842, 136 licensed taverns operated in Kingston to serve a population of 9,000. City officials saw fit to pass a bylaw to restrain and punish "Drunkards, Mendicants and Street Beggars."

Was it surprising that some residents and officials believed that the poor were also suffering from insanity? Why else would they behave in such a manner? Toronto architect John Howard first broached the idea of an asylum for Kingston as early as 1829. At that time the mentally ill were simply tossed into county jails like criminals. In 1830 the House of Assembly in the province of Upper Canada took the first step to differentiate between criminals and the mentally ill when it authorized "provisions for the relief of lunatics." However, it took another 11 years before the government initiated separate accommodations.

Kingston and Toronto were considered the likeliest candidates for such accommodations. Kingston had a population of 5,000; Toronto had a population of 13,000. Toronto won the deal.

At that time, a wealthy man by the name of John Solomon Cartwright was struck with the "Italian Villa" craze that had taken Kingston by storm. Cartwright built Rockwood Villa in 1841, in a style described by historian as Tuscan and Neo-Baroque. The centre of the house was an octagonal rotunda that extended up two floors, surrounded by a balcony at the second level, and crowned by a panelled dome containing a rose-glass skylight. Unfortunately, Cartwright died in 1844. A Mr. John Palmer Litchfield, thought to be a former inspector of hospitals in South Australia and the former medical superintendent of the Walton Asylum in Liverpool, rented the house in 1854, with the intention of turning it into a hospital.

Now Litchfield was quite a scoundrel, a con artist and, at the very least, was definitely of dubious character. Litchfield had at one time worked as a newspaper reporter in Europe and used this career to slip into outpatient clinics in London. Once there he masqueraded as a medical student, observing and learning enough about medical procedures to "get by" in any technical conversation.

It was reported that he had been imprisoned in Australia when it was discovered by the Australian lieutenant-governor that "Dr." Litchfield had no medical degree. Financial support for Litchfield's own hospital was withdrawn, which left him unable to pay his accounts and subject to a jail term. Nevertheless, he managed to leave Australia and head to Canada.

Upon landing in Canada, Litchfield was introduced to Sir John A. MacDonald, who was instrumental in his later appointment as medical superintendent of the Rockwood Asylum in Kingston. When he arrived in Kingston in 1854, Litchfield busied himself as one of the six men who were developing a medical school at Queen's University. He actually billed himself as an instructor of midwifery and forensic medicine. He was biding his time while the province of Upper Canada was preparing to license and finance an asylum in Kingston.

In October 1856 the government finally agreed and approximately 35 acres of the Cartwright estate, including the buildings, were purchased by the crown for an asylum for the criminally insane. Since money was not immediately forthcoming, the stables were temporarily renovated to take in 24 women from the penitentiary. The stables were converted into rooms measuring 2.75 by 1.5 metres (9 by 5 feet). The only light entered through barred windows, and the patients slept on straw.

By September 1859 construction of a new building was under way. Up to 100 convicts handled almost all the aspects of the construction. The asylum was built with a view of Lake Ontario, as this was thought to have a calming effect on patients. It was built chiefly from limestone and had a tin roof. The following year Litchfield reported 40 new prisoners living in the completed east wing of the building. The female patients were still housed in the horse stables and that remained the case until 1868.

A diary kept by a caretaker named Evans read: "Their meat was cut into small bits and they ate with a spoon or with their fingers as they chose. Tin pint cups took the place of bowls. Straw ticks and straw pillows made up the bedding.

"[The new asylum] was first lighted with coal oil lamps, one at each end of the ward. With the first two medical superintendents, we had no such thing as nicely painted walls and ceilings."

A year after the completion of the asylum, Litchfield boasted about how the death rate among patients had dropped from 7 to 3.5 percent.

With an eye to progress, Litchfield decided to expand and proposed that special accommodations be prepared for patients of a higher class, as was the custom in other countries. He also wanted to turn the stables into a home for 40 or 50 mentally challenged children.

Litchfield's favourite treatment for patients was "a bottle of the best Scotch Ale or Dublin Stout, a medicine that will bear repetition with the best results and no straight-jacket in the world will contribute better to quietness and repose."

The public of Kingston, even the wealthiest families, inquired about admittance despite the fact that the hospital was intended only for the criminally insane. Prominent Kingston families could bypass this technicality by first having their mentally ill relatives incarcerated in local jails.

Litchfield's life ended in 1868 at the age of 60. He was still holding the position of medical superintendent. His charade was only uncovered by Thomas Bibson, a Queen's professor, in the 1940s. Bibson traced Litchfield's background and found his qualifications were completely fabricated.

Dr. John Robinson Dickson, the personal physician of John A. MacDonald, was appointed the new superintendent. Dickson attempted to rid the asylum of poor attendants and introduce a new order to the system. His work was hampered by a politically appointed assistant who believed, among other things, that good treatment involved shaving blocks of wood to different thicknesses, according to the phases of the moon!

Superintendent Dickson was instrumental in having an act passed which made Rockwood Insane Asylum available for the general public. The name of the place changed to The Asylum for the Insane.

In 1878 Dr. William Metcalf arrived as the next superintendent. He was faced with barren wards, filthy straw beds, stinking urinals, and patients who were still confined to windowless cells in the basement. There were a total of 390 patients under the care and supervision of 14 attendants. Metcalf began a series of reforms and ended the practice of using wristlets (handcuff-like shackles) and muffs (two hands bound in one boxing glove) as a means of restraint.

In 1888 a school for psychiatric nurses opened at the hospital, and in 1895, formal lectures in psychiatry were established at Queen's University. In 1907 the name of the facility became The Rockwood Hospital, and in 1920 it became the Ontario Hospital, Kingston. In the 1930s a travelling Mental Health Clinic was established, as well as a series of halfway houses for recovering patients upon their release. Although it fell into disorganization during the Second World War, the clinic was revived in 1946.

Today, the Kingston Psychiatric Hospital is closed.

Archives of Ontario

Kingston, South Cottage for Women at Rockwood Asylum circa 1900. A slow start, perhaps, but a great improvement over their last quarters — the horse stables!

Many of the buildings in this city are made of limestone. The beginnings of the city were rocky, too, with wars and forts, plagues, prisoners, and the questionable treatment of the mentally ill. Despite all that, when you visit Kingston today, you get a solid feeling of antiquity, of charm and beauty, and of its wild and fascinating history.

Lake Superior Sites

Water is the womb of Mother Earth and Lake Superior is the largest inland lake in the world. To travel there is the return to our original state, an experience of rebirth. Anyone who has camped, canoed, or hiked the shoreline or interior of the region knows this feeling. The haunting roar of waves, crashing to shore, stirs the soul. The breathtaking sunsets, streaking across sky and water, paint unforgettable pictures of peace and grandeur. In those moments you are rendered whole.

Lake Superior has many faces. The weather is not consistent nor is the temperament of the lake. Each trip is different, and special. Favourite haunts for many are Batchawana Bay, Pancake Bay, and Lake Superior Provincial Park.

Batchawana Bay is located about 56 kilometres (35 miles) northwest of Sault Ste. Marie on the northern shore of Lake Superior. A small community named Batchawana, including a Native reserve, marks the shoreline first. The name Batchawana is derived from the Native word "obatchiwanang" meaning "at the current of the strait." Batchawana Bay Provincial Day Park and Information Centre will introduce you to the vast beaches of light sand and sweeping waves, as well as to the resorts, where excellent dining and rental accommodations are available.

A few kilometres north is Pancake Bay Provincial Park. This park takes its name from a custom of the early voyageurs. Travelling the Lake Superior waters from Fort William to Montreal, their canoes laden with furs, they would stop over at the site of the present park. Here they would

Archives of Ontario

Lake Superior circa 1930s. Early tourists attempt the precarious drive to Thunder Bay.

finish their remaining flour supplies before reaching Sault Ste. Marie, where they would restock. Pancakes were the order of the day!

Sharply contrasting the rugged, rocky coast that predominates on Lake Superior, Batchewana Bay and Pancake Bay both have fine sandy beaches. Protected between promontories, the prevailing winds, currents, and waves have resulted in accumulations of pure sand in each of these bays. To camp at Pancake Bay is to be lulled to sleep by the music of Lake Superior.

Only another hour north of Pancake there is yet another amazing park. It is 1,170 square kilometres (520 miles) of natural beauty of every description.

Convulsed by earthquakes, gouged by ice-age glaciers, blanketed in parts by volcanic lavas, Lake Superior Provincial Park presents a scenic grandeur of high hills and steep-walled valleys, as well as rivers, beaches, and smooth-rolled stones. The park is truly a magical place of raw natural energy. Native legends are tightly woven into the fabric of this park.

The first Europeans encountered a wilderness full of life and clear, fresh water. Early explorers often remarked about the beauty and natural state of the land left intact through thousands of years of Native occupation. A small band of Ojibwa hunters, fishers, and gatherers claimed the Agawa Valley. There, two main villages were located at Sinclair Cove and near the Agawa River mouth. Several smaller camps existed upriver and on the inland lakes. To the Ojibwa, Lake Superior and its shoreline were, and still are, metaphors for spiritual growth and movement — a place where one can stand at the threshold of many worlds — physical and mystical, ancient and modern, civilized and wild, earthly and otherworldly.

A rare example of this is Agawa Rock, an impressive and haunting spot, a sheer rock that rises to tower above the cold, clear waters of Lake Superior. Ancient rock paintings left by the Native medicine people of yesterday adorn this powerful place where the earth's energies are exposed. These rock paintings, or pictographs as they are called, are attributed to Ojibwa shaman artists. It was here the medicine people handled spiritual matters, conducted rituals, and worked to provide a link between this world and the spirit world, a place of power.

Archeologists believe the art at Agawa Rock dates back hundreds or even thousands of years. The study of the water level of Lake Superior, which was above the pictographs prior to three thousand years ago, provides conclusive evidence of their considerable age. Back in the early 1970s, archaeologists explored the area and conducted site surveys of the park. Several dozen archaeological sites were discovered. Native villages and campsites, burial grounds, three rock-art sites, a Hudson's Bay Company trading post site, and several sacred sites were located. Artifacts uncovered in the park represented more than three thousand years of Native settlement.

Natives rendered these glyphs for a variety of reasons. Much of the rock art depicts images of religious experiences gained during vision quests, group ceremonies, and the acknowledgement of spiritual assistance.

In 1990 Julie and Thor Conway, an archaeologist and anthropologist team, worked with two Ojibwa medicine people from the Garden River band. The Natives helped them to better understand the meaning of the glyphs and of the mysteries they contain. It was discovered that many of the pictograph sites in Ontario refer to birds of prey and many appear on vertical cliffs that drop into a body of water. Each site was given a name. The shamans, it was revealed, regarded large nesting birds on cliffs as metaphors for the presence of unseen thunderbirds. According to Julie and Thor, "Thunderbirds, or Animkeeg, represent tremendous power. As birds, they travel in the heavens between the earth and the spirit world. Ravens, various hawks, and eagles continue to nest at many rock-art sites, as they did in the past."

Ka-Gaw-Gee-Wabikong, or "Raven Rock White Cliff Beside the Water," refers to the white wash from bird droppings that can be seen below active nesting sites. There are, however, also white mineral deposits on the cliff faces which are calcite solutions caused by minerals dissolved in rain water. Medicine people consider these deposits to be indications of unseen nests of cliff-dwelling thunderbirds. These calcite deposits are visible at Agawa Rock.

The Conways have studied the Agawa site for 17 years and recorded 17 paintings. A pictograph of a faint thunderbird was found as recently as 1989.

The most famous rock-art painting in Canada is located here in the park at Agawa Rock. The pictograph is entitled "Michipeshu," which means "the great cat." Michipeshu has lynx-like tuffs of fur sticking out from his cheeks and dragon-like spines running the length of his back and tail. According to legend, Michipeshu is a metaphor for Lake Superior — powerful, mysterious, and very dangerous. Although the creature lives underwater with the other giant serpents, some Natives view the dragon-like spines on the back and tail as horns of power, while others believe them to be legs. There is certainly a sense of power here.

This sacred land gave visions to the Natives, but why did they record them and leave them behind? Were they to be a record, an inspiration, a reminder? Or is there a message being given? Thousands of people today visit these areas in pursuit of personal visions or perhaps even for a sense of history. There definitely is power here, and maybe the possibility of touching your own power, of touching your essential and authentic self.

Lindsay

Many of the villages, towns, and cities in Ontario are named after places in other countries, are named in honour of royalty, or are variations of the Native place-name. Few are given as a result of a gunshot wound to the leg.

Prior to the arrival of settlers, the Mississauga Nation in the mid-1700s camped at East Cross Creek. An Irishman named Patrick O'Connell was the first white settler to take up residence, on Lot 7, Concession 2, on the west shore of Scugog River, in 1825. Close behind O'Connell came William Purdy and his two sons, Jesse and Hazard, in 1827. This family left much for history!

The Purdys had entered into a contract with the Canadian government to build a sawmill and a ten-foot dam on the Scugog River by the year 1828. A gristmill was to be completed by the following year. For this they were to receive 400 acres and a bonus of $600.

The dam and sawmill were completed in September 1828. The townspeople waited expectantly for the millpond to fill up. Some thought it would do so within 24 hours, but the water failed to reach the top of the dam until the following April. Then, during the spring, pressure on the dam was too great, the centre timbers shifted on the rocky bottom of the river, and the dam was swept away. The Purdys required a time extension from the government and it was granted. Not until April, 1830, was the dam rebuilt and the gristmill completed.

In the early 1830s, William Purdy took a stand against the Family Compact, the small group of wealthy Loyalists who comprised the governing class at that time. This led to William's arrest and transport to the Cobourg jail. After several days he was released and told to mind his own business. Shortly thereafter, in 1837, William Purdy and his son Jesse moved to Bath and left Hazard Purdy in charge of the mill. In 1844 Hazard sold the mill and the 400-acre Purdy tract of land to Hiram Bigelow.

Before Hazard left Lindsay, he was confronted with a series of problems resulting from the dam his family had constructed. Apparently, the Purdy dam had altered the geography of the land. It was responsible for the flooding of approximately 60,000 acres. Most of the forest and surrounding vegetation turned to swamp and a plague of swamp fever resulted. The flooding was blamed for many deaths. Hostility mounted, and a determined group of farmers from adjacent townships, armed with flintlocks, pitchforks, and axes, marched to Purdy Mills and hacked away a portion of the dam. Hazard did rebuild it, but at a lower level. The year after he left, 1844, the Purdy dam was torn down and replaced by a new dam and a lock to facilitate the navigation between Sturgeon Lake and Scugog Lake. At that point the settlement was called Purdy Mills.

The originally surveyed townsite was covered in greater part by a dense cedar swamp. In 1835 Jeremiah Britton came, together with his sons Charles and Wellington, from Port Hope to settle on 100 acres of land at what is now the foot of Kent Street. There, he built a log structure and opened a tavern. A notice posted over his bar read, KEEP SOBER OR KEEP AWAY. James Hutton arrived in 1837 and opened the first store in town.

In 1834 John Houston of Cavan, and a small party of men, arrived at Lots 20 and 21 in the 5th Concession of Ops Township to plot out a town. One of Houston's assistants, a man named Lindsay, was accidentally wounded in the leg by a gunshot. Unfortunately for him, infection set in and he died. The survey crew buried Lindsay on the bank of the Scugog River at what is now MacDonnell Park. The name Lindsay was marked on the plan and was later adopted as the official town name.

Virgin wilderness still surrounded the tiny settlement; sometimes deer were seen drinking from the river in the heart of the village or running from wolves up Kent Street. The village grew slowly but steadily. Kent Street was chopped out of the swamp in 1840, and other streets followed. By the year 1851, about 300 settlers called Lindsay their home.

Every community had at least one colourful character who attracted a great deal of attention in his or her day. Lindsay resident Dan MacDonald was such a person. Dan was a storekeeper who operated a business on Kent Street. His claim to fame was physical strength — enough to lift a 272-kilogram (600 pound) barrel of flour. He also fascinated folks by juggling a 45-kilogram (100 pound) dumbbell. As fate would have it, poor Dan overestimated his ability. He attempted to lift a 727-kilogram (1,600 pound) piece of machinery; he broke a blood vessel in the process and it did him in. The citizens, not wanting to forget this daring and colourful man, inscribed the following on his tombstone:

> *"Ye weak beware!*
> *There lies the strong*
> *A victim to his strength*
> *He lifted sixteen hundred pounds*
> *And here he lies at length."*

In 1854 a charter had been granted for the construction of a railway from Port Hope to Lindsay. By 1857 the railway had reached town. It was later extended to Beaverton and eventually Midland. With the coming of the railway, the town entered a period of rapid expansion, and an application was made to the legislature to incorporate the town. Lindsay became an incorporated town on June 10, 1857. The population at this time was 1,100.

Few towns escape the harsh reality of fire. Lindsay experienced such a fate in 1861, when fire swept through the town destroying four hotels, two mills, the post office, and 83 other buildings. The Purdy homestead, built in 1830, was one of the buildings lost. The homeless numbered 400. Despite the hardships, the town remained without adequate fire protection until 1892, when the Waterworks Company was formed.

In those days the townsfolk loved to attend the opera house for a night of gaiety and relaxation. For years the opera house was situated on the upper floor of the town hall, which had been constructed in 1863. The town and its citizens wanted a new opera house, and in 1892 began construction of one at the end of the main street. The famous Canadian actress, Marie Dressler, made her debut at age five, right there at the

Lindsay Opera House. She later achieved fame as a much-loved character actress and played the role of Tugboat Annie in a series of movies. Today the Academy Theatre is a beautifully preserved building and is still a cornerstone for live entertainment.

In 1901 Lindsay was blessed by a generous contribution from millionaire James Ross for the construction of a hospital. He did this in memory of his parents, who had been residents of Lindsay.

Here is a strange and little-known tale about our town of Lindsay. There was a bullfight — right here. Imagine the excitement! Apparently, the promoters of the event went to great lengths to ensure an authentic Mexican fight. They even imported the bulls from Mexico. Many shocked citizens openly opposed the fight and loudly protested their concerns across the country. Nevertheless, the promoters continued, promising this affair to be a bloodless fight, and they went to great lengths to ensure this. It was assured that the matadors would use only wooden swords. In August 1958 people flocked to Lindsay to watch their first, and perhaps only, bullfight. The event began with disappointment: the first bull refused to fight, and had to be lured out of the arena by a heifer. The other bulls did, however, put on a spectacular show. There was even an enraged bull, who charged the town's chief of police when he strode into the arena for a symbolic "kill." The chief ran to safety just in the nick of time!

Although spectators appeared to enjoy the day, the promoters reported they lost money because hundreds of people crashed the gate.

Lindsay today is often frequented by boaters. It is the "Gateway to the Kawarthas," in close proximity to Sturgeon Lake, Pigeon Lake, Lake Scugog, and the Scugog River, which is a vital link to the Trent Waterway Systems. Towns like Lindsay will continue to be viable because of their attraction to outdoor enthusiasts. Their state of the art fall fair, live theatre, historic past, and scenic downtown all foretell a strong and rosy future. Gunshot wounds and bullfights will remain tales for this town to tell.

Madoc

The discovery of gold near Madoc in 1866 touched off a gold rush equal to that in California or Alaska. Unlike other mining centres, Madoc was well-established before gold fever struck.

The village, situated 40 kilometres (25 miles) north of Belleville, was named after Madoc ad Owaiin Gwynedd, a legendary Welsh prince who was said to have discovered America in 1170. Prior to that lofty accomplishment, Madoc was the site of a Mohawk village. According to Native oral tradition, a party of Mississaugas left what is today Trenton for Lake Chuncall in Madoc as part of a plan to drive the Mohawks out of Ontario. A large battle ensued, and the Mississaugas defeated the Mohawks. Historians also tell us that because the lake was so small, the fish fed on human remains after the battle.

Donald Mackenzie, the founder of Madoc, arrived in the early 1830s and set about to build a saw mill and a gristmill. For the next 20 years the community was called Mackenzie's Mills, then Hastings, and finally Madoc.

In 1835 Uriah Seymour and John G. Pendergast opened an ironworks in Madoc that eventually employed 100 people. The company enjoyed success at first, but the difficulties of transportation and the lack of proper fuel forced it to close down in 1845. Ten years later, an energetic entrepreneur came along, hired 200 workers, and reopened the ironworks. Five years after that, the industry employed 500 villagers.

Madoc became a lucrative trading centre on the Hastings Road. The village, in the early 1860s, boasted four carriage shops, five blacksmith shops, two cabinet shops, a tannery, a watchmaker, and an organ company. The population of the community reached 900 by the year 1865. A year later Madoc's population and development would burst at the seams.

The idea of instant wealth has long haunted the dreams of man and driven many in search of gold. Marcus Powell, a division court clerk and part-time prospector, was no different. He had a hunch that he would strike the big one! On August 15, 1866, Powell, along with an old miner named Snider, went in search of the rainbow and its pot of gold. Searching high and low on John Richardson's farm, the men made a discovery; they thought they had found copper. Their disappointment quickly turned to elation when they were told that what they had actually found, on lot 18 of the 5th Concession, was gold! Word of the discovery remained a secret for a short time but, with available gold running 22 karats pure, the story was bound to get out.

Mr. Lyman Moon, a hotel proprietor who also drove the stagecoach, went to Belleville with the gold samples to discuss the formation of a mining company. The news was out, and hundreds of people began to arrive in the area. New hotels could not be built fast enough to accommodate these prospective millionaires. According to newspaper accounts, 2,000 people were expected from Prince Edward County alone. Eight thousand Chinese from the California goldfields were thought to be on their way. Madoc was in newspapers and magazines across Europe. The village population of 900 expanded rapidly to 5,000. The government became concerned for the safety of those 5,000 and declared the area under federal jurisdiction. On April 15, 1866, a mounted police squad of 25 men arrived in Madoc. Their job was to enforce the peace and attempt to monitor the 300 mines that would soon be operating in the area. Everybody was digging for gold.

The discovery of gold on the Richardson's farm gave birth to another village, Eldorado. Prior to the discovery of gold, only the Orange Hall, dating back to the 1840s, and the township hall, erected in the 1850s, stood at the site of the present hamlet.

Madoc and Eldorado soon attracted the likes of Caribou Cameron, a colourful character who had come from the goldfields of California and the Caribou. John Angus Cameron was born in Summerstown, Ontario, in 1820. A descendant of one of Glengarry's pioneer families, he had spent many years in the Caribou fields of British Columbia, prospecting for gold. He was reputed to have earned $250,000 in the Caribou when he sold his claim. At that time he employed 80 men, to whom he paid $10 to $16 a day. When Caribou Cameron left the Madoc area, he had accumulated another $15,000.

Cameron's wife, whose family lived in Cornwall, Ontario, had accompanied him to the Yukon, and she had died a short time later. To satisfy her dying wish, to be buried in Cornwall, Caribou Cameron accompanied her coffin by dog sled and pack train, and, finally, by ship around Cape Horn. When the ship arrived in New York, the customs officials did not believe his story — that the coffin was lead-lined and filled with whiskey to preserve the body. They opened the coffin to discover the body beautifully preserved and dressed as she had been when she died, several months before. This man had quite a history all of his own.

Although most of the gold mines in the area failed due to the difficulty and expense of extracting gold, other mineral deposits were discovered, including copper, lead, marble, talc, and lithographic stone. In 1869 a quartz mill was opened, which provided employment to area residents. The mine with the most continuous operation today is a talc mine, operated by Canada Talc Industries, which produces the only pure white talc in Canada. There is also a marble factory north of Highway 7 that makes chips for terrazzo flooring.

One might have expected Madoc to become a ghost town after the rush, but some prospectors remained and the village began to grow, thanks to the construction of the Belleville and North Hastings Railway and a gravel road south to Belleville.

Fire struck Madoc in 1873 and destroyed much of the village. Residents rallied and quickly rebuilt. Three years later the population was at 1,000. A short time later, the iron mines closed and the new railway system from Toronto to Ottawa went through Ivanhoe instead of Madoc, causing a change in population. The decline of the lumber trade was also responsible for lowering the population. In the 1930s the construction of Highway 7 gave the village an east–west link, and this encouraged some new growth.

Archives of Ontario

Madoc Talc Mine circa 1909. This mine is still operating but gone are the mules, and the pits are now deep in the earth.

During the last 20 years, Madoc has attracted hundreds of amateur geologists and prospectors, searching the countryside for gems (even diamonds), and, of course, gold. A renewed interest in precious and semi-precious stones has put the whole area back on the map. Anyone wishing to be a millionaire could take a trip from Madoc to Bancroft and stop many times along the way to test their luck.

Marmora

It seems that Crowe Lake knew it had something to crow about —
a huge marble rock. Marmora is a town and a township, named to
commemorate that rock. *Marmora* is the latin plural for "marble."

Thirty miles north of the city of Belleville is the site of Ontario's
first mining operation. It was Charles Hayes, along with his wife, who
set sail from Ireland in 1820 to follow a dream. The dream was to
establish the first ironworks in Upper Canada and become the first
industrialist in this new land.

Hayes and his wife docked in New York before travelling up the
Hudson River and the Mohawk Valley to Sacketts Harbour. From there
they voyaged to Montreal to meet with Peter McGill, a financier, and then
went on to Kingston, Ontario. The Hayes left Kingston and proceeded
northwest until they came to a narrows in the Crowe River, about 160
kilometres (100 miles) hence. It was here that this entrepreneur eventually
built the first company town in Upper Canada. It was a formidable task
when you consider that Hayes had been a linen merchant back home,
albeit a successful one. He was to start the first wave of industrialism,
but not the last. Hayes had obtained an order-in-council to give him the
authority to establish the colony's first industrial location, and Marmora
had all the right ingredients for the making of iron ore.

Marmora Township was surveyed in 1821 and attached to Hastings
County. A 24-kilometre (15 mile) road was constructed from Sidney
Township to Marmora, and by 1824 the population of the township
had reached 400.

Marmora, not to mention the surrounding area, was laden with iron ore. This mineral is the fourth-most plentiful element in the earth. The quality of iron is dependent on the concentration of hematite and magnetite and on the ability of the iron-master to separate them from the waste rock in which they are found. The smelting of this ore has been done for more than 3,000 years. Early smelting involved charcoal fires and bellows in the production of a spongy mass called a bloom. Then it was discovered that greater heat resulted in the extraction of higher quality iron. Ironmasters created narrow, truncated, pyramid furnaces for the purpose of heating the rock.

Hayes knew that Marmora was the right place, because iron ore was present 4 kilometres (.25 miles) to the north, on the surface of the banks of the Crowe River. Another site, now Blairton, revealed a mountain of ore available for the process. Limestone, also to be found in the area, could be used as a flux. The endless forest there would fuel the blast furnaces, and the river itself would provide the power to drive the water wheels that pumped the bellows to intensify the blast.

In less than two years, Hayes had the first blast furnace in operation. A road had been built, and the firebricks, furnace equipment, and workers arrived to settle the village of Marmora and begin work at the new ironworks. Andre Philpot, author of *A Species of Adventure*, highlights this spectacular accomplishment. He writes:

> The completed works presented one solid mass of building of limestone, constructed on the face of a bank of the same material, 40 feet high [12 metres] to the level of the bank. The fires were blasted by bellows driven by six enormous water wheels, harnessed to the river. At the heart of the community was the furnace complex. All day the villagers would tend and feed its needs. At night, the flames would shoot up from the chimney heads lighting up the valley. All the time, the grinding of the water wheels and the pumping of the bellows reminded the Village of why it was there.

Hayes completed the construction of a second furnace in 1825. The interior diameter of the structure was approximately three metres (8.5 to 9 feet), and its height was nine metres (30 feet). A pair of German bellows, each 8.5 metres (28 feet) long and 4.5 metres (15 feet) wide, were used in the operation. Philpot adds:

> For each furnace, the whole mechanism was connected to a water wheel, the larger of which was reported to be 8.1 metres [27 feet] in diameter and 1.8 metres [6 feet] wide. The wheels drove shafts and the shafts pumped the bellows to intensity the fires. These furnaces faced onto a common casting house built of limestone. Here, the molten iron would be led off into channels dug into the sand floor guttermen. For the main channel, bar-shaped moulds would branch off, and the whole shape reminded the workers of piglets feeding on a sow. Hence the basic produce was labeled "pig iron."

Three charcoal houses were situated on a ledge to the east of the works. These buildings had a total capacity of 200,000 bushels. One ton of iron required 300 bushels of charcoal for fire.

The ironworks was a major source of iron ballast. In those days ships still required ballast weight in order to keep things on an even keel.

By 1824, a gristmill, a sawmill, a brake mill, a carpenter's shop, a bake house, a counting house, three charcoal houses, two ore kilns, and a potashery were established in this ironworks community.

Charles Hayes was a man willing to spend his own money to attain success; the government of the time was not so committed. Hayes knew, by the end of 1822, that he was spending most of his fortune in operation costs and roadwork to get his product to market. Water transportation was the answer. He knew that although the Crowe River was impassable to the south of the village, a canal was feasible. Hayes could envision a canal from Crowe Lake to the Trent River. It was a 19-kilometre (12 mile) stretch through the bush, and he was willing to spend some of his own money on the canal project if the government would approve and assist in the idea. The Trent River canal system did not get started for two more decades, but Hayes could see where things were going. The government, unfortunately, had no intention of assisting Hayes to build a canal. His debts overcame his dream, and in September 1824 he ceded his property and industry to the trustees. In the end the creditors even possessed his household furniture. Hayes returned to Ireland a broken man, and in April 1830 he wrote, "Thus you see it is not always the person who had done the most service [who] is most likely to be rewarded, for I cannot help saying that I think I have done more good to Upper Canada than any other individual that was in it ..."

It was his associate and financier Peter McGill who took over the operations of the ironworks. He, too, was riddled with problems of transportation, and he attempted to sell the ironworks in 1826 and 1827, but found no buyers. In 1831 the ironworks closed its doors. The first wave was over.

By 1837 a commission was appointed by the government to investigate the possibility of moving the penitentiary from Kingston to Marmora. Although consideration was given to running the ironworks with convict labour, the idea was abandoned once again due to transportation difficulties.

In 1847 Van Norman purchased the ironworks. An experienced ironmaster himself, he, too, was defeated by the expense of shipping his product and abandoned the operation in 1854 with his resources depleted. Another wave in Marmora's history.

The subsequent closing of the ironworks stunted the growth of the village for many years, and farming and lumbering took over as the mainstay of the economy. When gold was discovered in the vicinity in the 1860s, it was an entirely new enterprise and a big relief to the populace. From 1873 to 1880, gold mining was carried out by the Gatling Gold and Silver Mining Company, but was later sold when the operations proved once again to be too expensive.

By 1878 the population of Marmora stood at 400. A sawmill, a carding and woollen factory, and a gristmill provided some employment for the villagers. B.C. Hubbell operated a dry goods, a grocery, a footwear and a furniture store, as well as the undertaking service for the area in 1888.

A terrible fire in Marmora in 1900 destroyed the main business district and forced the relocation of many businesses. The following year Marmora was incorporated as a village.

It was the 20th century that saw the mining of iron ore regain its importance, when the Marmoraton Mines (part of the American Bethlehem Steel Corporation) went into operation nearby. Millions of tons of limestone were stripped from the top of large magnetic beds to permit open-pit mining. A sintering plant was set up at the company's mills in New York State. The company produced up to 1,500 tons of concentrate daily at the peak of the plant's activity. The mining operations were closed in the late 1970s.

One wonders what new wave will bring a swell to the economy of the community with the big, marble stone.

Muskoka

Muskoka's pristine lakes, islands of gnarled pines, and rugged, remote beaches pull people to their shores like a great magnet.

In the early 1800s, few people knew Muskoka existed. Only small, wandering bands of Ojibwa traversed this region for hunting. What a magnificent hunting ground!

The wealth of the forests called the first settlers. Hardworking lumberjacks harvested white pine, and pioneer farmers cleared the land. There was no time, then, for recreation!

The first holidayers to head here arrived sometime in the 1860s. Getting there was part of the adventure. First by railway, then by steamboat, rowboat, and finally by foot, they arrived at what was to become Gravenhurst.

It was an arduous journey and there was no one to greet them, but they revelled in the rugged, wild scenery, the fresh air and the clear waters. Local hospitality was simple but genuine. Visitors were truly impressed — enough to want to come back, and even more joined them to explore this rugged land.

Getting there remained a problem for many years. No reliable means of transportation to Ontario's central lake district existed in the 1800s. A.P. Cockburn, the area representative in government, recognized this shortcoming. He envisioned the possibility of water transportation opening up the district and persuaded the government to install a lock at Port Carling to connect Lakes Muskoka and Rosseau, and to dig a channel at Port Standfield to connect Lakes Rosseau and Joseph.

Gravenhurst circa 1900. Later known as the Garner Lodge, this was home to many weddings like the one here of Bertha Mickle and Howard Cane.

An ambitious entrepreneur, Cockburn proceeded to build a fleet of steamers for the lakes — large, powerful boats with native names like *Sagamo* and *Segwun*. He worked to get a railway to the lakehead at Gravenhurst by 1875.

In 1886 the railway went on to Huntsville. Captain Marsh, a transportation magnate, took the lead and put steamers on the upper lakes: Vernon, Fairy, Peninsula, Mary, and Lake of Bays. This helped to open Muskoka to the major commercial centres of the south.

Resorts sprang up around the district. Pratt's Rosseau House was followed by such well-known places as Summit House, Clevelands House, Windermere House, and the Royal Muskoka Hotel on the southern lakes. On the northern lakes there was Deerhurst Resort, Britannia Hotel, Wawa Hotel, Bigwin Inn and others.

The buildings were typically three-storeyed with gables, turrets, and wide, wrap-around verandas where guests lounged in wicker chairs and sipped refreshments.

Gravenhurst

The town of Gravenhurst, situated at the south end of Lake Muskoka, was named by a Canadian postmaster general in 1861. The first settler to arrive here was James McCabe, who built a tavern at the site in 1859.

The settlement of Gravenhurst grew at a rapid pace thanks to Peter Cockburn, who began a lumbering business in 1865–66. Cockburn was responsible for making Gravenhurst a lake port when he launched the *Wenonah*, the first steamer on Lake Muskoka, in 1866. The community expanded after the Free Grants Act of 1868, when settlers flocked to the area to take advantage of free land. By the 1870s, Gravenhurst could boast it was the mill capital of Northern Ontario, or "Sawdust City" as it was otherwise known. At one time a total of 17 mills operated in the area. A thousand saw blades helped to carve out an economy. According to the *Toronto World* of July 13, 1887, Gravenhurst had four churches, a library, a school, a town hall, a telephone exchange, a bank, a foundry, a ginger-ale bottling works, many fine stores, and four hotels.

Dougald Brown, who had previously built the Steamboat and Stage House Hotel in 1867, founded Brown's Beverages in 1873. This company is the oldest continuing industry in the community. Two years later Gravenhurst was incorporated as a village.

Gravenhurst was booming, but tragedy came in the guise of fire! On the blustery night of September 22, 1887, between midnight and one o'clock in the morning, a fire started at Mowry and Sons foundry on Muskoka Road, just north of the present-day post office. By the time the alarm was sounded, the whole building was ablaze, and it spread quickly to Brignall's wagon shop and home. The residents of Gravenhurst rallied to the scene with a horse-drawn engine but, unfortunately, the men had difficulty operating the pumps and by the time they got things rolling, the fire had reached the four-storey Fraser House Hotel. By then, things were really out of control. The wind carried burning debris across the streets, and the fire spread to all of the wooden buildings in the business section of town. Burning cinders rained upon Gravenhurst, setting a dozen different buildings ablaze.

A telegraph appeal went out to Bracebridge, Orillia, and Barrie requesting help. The Barrie brigades loaded their equipment onto the nearest railway handcars, but it was too late. As if things weren't bad enough, the ammunition stocked in stores began to explode. A towering inferno raged for three long hours, until nothing was left. It was all over by daybreak. The buildings destroyed totalled 50, including the Anglican Church and a brand new public school.

The citizens of Gravenhurst did rebuild, this time using stone or brick as a building material. The Fire Department was also upgraded.

Tuberculosis (TB), commonly called consumption, was prevalent in the 1890s. No one knew the cause and the mortality rate was high. The treatment recommended was rest, good nutrition, and fresh, clean air. The Muskokas seemed to be the perfect place to establish a sanatorium. In 1896 Sir William James Gage began the construction of a sanatorium on the east shore of Muskoka Bay, just north of Gravenhurst. The following year, the Muskoka Cottage Sanatorium opened its doors and welcomed 35 tuberculosis patients. It was the first such dwelling of its kind in Canada.

Business was brisk and expansion began; capacity reached 100 patients. Those in the early stages of the disease were admitted at rates of $12 to $15 per week, in 1910. If conditions required a stay-in bed, an extra dollar per day was levied. The sanatorium looked more like a posh hotel, and brochures implied that patients would require only a few months of Muskoka's clean, healthy air before returning to home and work.

In 1902 The Muskoka Free Hospital for Consumptives was built. It was a welcome addition to Ontario tuberculosis facilities. This title certainly implied that other TB hospitals were not "free." Unfortunately, the original infirmary and most of the central administration building burned down in November 1920. Nearby Massey Hall, a recreation centre for patients, was temporarily used for accommodation. In 1958 the province bought the premises and converted the site into the Ontario Fire College.

Cottages with open fronts enclosed by windows were often constructed to house TB patients. Tents also played some part in the treatment of the disease. Many of these shelters lacked any significant heat source but were occupied during cool temperatures in spring and fall. Many believed that if breathing fresh air didn't kill the germs, maybe freezing them would.

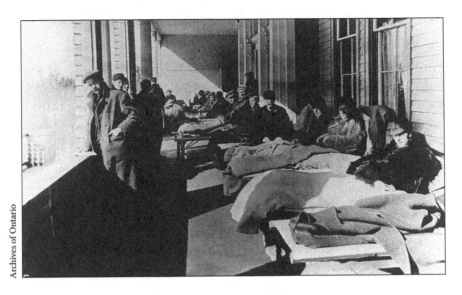

Archives of Ontario

Muskoka, Gravenhurst, circa 1900. The Muskokas were thought to be the best place for sanatoriums — lots of fresh, clean air.

In 1916, the Calydor Sanatorium brought the number of TB treatment centres along Muskoka Bay up to four. It was Dr. C.D. Parfitt who persuaded a group of investors to construct a new centre for the treatment of private patients. During the 1930s the provincial government handled the cost of TB treatment, but the depression and subsequent restriction of funds closed Calydor in 1935.

1939 marked the beginning of the Second World War, and as the number of German prisoners of war increased, Britain soon arranged for prisoner confinement in Canada. In June 1940 the Calydor Sanatorium was renamed Camp 20 and used for the imprisonment of German officers and soldiers.

Guard towers and barbed wire went up, and since the Calydor grounds were smaller than the Geneva Convention required for the number of prisoners, additional playing fields and gardens were acquired. Daily activities included marching, building stone walls, and fishing at a pier at Gull Lake Park. The German prisoners also presented frequent plays and concerts. Using their own instructors, they offered a variety of courses, up to and including university level, and were also able to study correspondence courses from Canadian universities.

In 1942 Wilhelm Bach, a German army major, died at Camp 20 and officials accorded him a full military funeral. His swastika-draped casket was transported by hearse to Mickle Memorial Cemetery. The funeral procession included a truckload of floral tributes — one of the largest came from Adolph Hitler.

In 1943 the second-largest prison-break from a Canadian camp took place at Camp 20. Seven German prisoners of war, shrouded in sheets that camouflaged them in the snow, made their break for freedom. Two were captured almost immediately as they crossed the final enclosure. Four others were captured that night and the next day near Barrie and Washago. One prisoner made good his escape to America.

Ironically, German prisoners were succeeded by Jewish vacationers when the Gateway Hotel opened in 1949. A decade later the property became a youth camp, which ultimately closed. Fire claimed the Calydor in November 1967.

Another landmark and social centre for many years in Gravenhurst was Sloan's Restaurant. Sloan's originated in April, 1915, when Archie and Sarah Sloan opened their confectionery and ice cream parlour on the west side of Muskoka Road. In those days customers sat on ice-cream chairs at small, round tables, and ordered sarsaparilla for 5 cents, a soda for 10 cents, or a marvelous two-scoop sundae submerged beneath rich toppings for 15 cents. The candy counter tempted with its licorice plugs, chocolate cigars and brooms, and various other confectionaries, each for only a penny.

In 1930 a youthful Gordon Sloan took over the business after the death of his father. In 1947 Sloan undertook a major renovation. He bought the grocery store then operated by Charles Tomlinson, joined it to the original restaurant, and created the Old Muskoka Room. Under his imaginative and energetic management, the revitalized Sloan's Restaurant prospered. Anyone travelling to the district had to stop in Gravenhurst to sample a piece of blueberry pie at Sloan's.

Sloan's Restaurant was later sold to Winchester Arms, a chain of restaurants operating in Ontario. The company renovated the building, but kept the traditional menu. During renovations the original recipe for Sloan's blueberry pie was discovered. Eventually this business closed.

Tourists and residents also attend the many concerts held at the popular opera hall and players' theatre built in 1897, and some considerable local talent has been spawned there.

Bracebridge

The town of Bracebridge, originally called North Falls, was renamed in 1864, with the establishment of the post office. It is possible that Bracebridge was named for Washington Irving's novel *Bracebridge Hall* or for a community in Lincolnshire, England. This picturesque town was settled in 1860, with the arrival of John Beal and David Leith.

Provincial Land Surveyor John Stoughton Dennis, acting on government instructions for surveyors, brought his party up the road to Muskoka Bay and proceeded by canoe to the site of Bracebridge in 1860. After a reconnaissance of the Muskoka River, and the country in the vicinity of North Falls (Bracebridge), J.S. Dennis came to the conclusion "that at no point to be found for miles on that branch did the same facilities exist for crossing the stream than immediately at the falls." Perhaps an easier townsite could have been chosen on more level land in the valley just to the west, but the river led to the falls, and the main road was to cross the falls. This made the location of the town's centre rough, hilly, and rugged but very quaint and picturesque. Three log huts were built on the north side of the falls within a year.

James Cooper and his brother, Robert, worked to continue the Muskoka Road from the south galls to the north falls. James held land on both sides of the falls. In 1864 he built a tavern while his son, Joseph, operated a sawmill. Alexander Bailey, who had acquired land from James Cooper north of the river, built a gristmill and sawmill at the foot of the falls.

Bracebridge benefitted from this ideal location on the river. It had ample water supply for power and transportation and soon grew into a thriving lumbering, manufacturing, and tourist centre. By 1868 the Ontario Legislature designated Bracebridge as the capital of the new Territorial District of Muskoka. Bracebridge was incorporated as a village in 1875. Two years later, the population rose to 1,600 and, in 1889, Bracebridge became a town.

In 1872 Henry James Bird erected a three-storey, clear-pine-framed woollen mill on the upper part of the north side of the falls at Bracebridge.

Bird had come to Bracebridge hoping that Muskoka would become a sheep-raising district. Prior to Bracebridge, Bird had operated a mill at Glen Allen, in Peel Township, Wellington County, near Guelph. That mill was flooded out by rising water levels in 1870 and 1871.

To support his business, Bird assisted settlers in the acquisition of flocks of sheep and the district became a centre for raising sheep. Muskoka lamb became so popular, it was sold to city markets and became an item on restaurant and dining room menus as far away as New York City.

On June 4, 1873, Bird married Miss Mary Matilda Ney of Glen Allen, and he and his bride made their home above the mill. After a few years of very brisk business, Bird and his wife set about planning a separate home for the family. His choice of design for the house, which became known as Woodchester Villa, was based on the home-building theories of the American author, lecturer, and phrenologist Orson H. Fowler. Fowler had published a book advocating the octagonal shape as a new superior mode of building. Fowler argued that an octagonal home was a more healthy home. Square buildings, he said, did not conform to the spherical forms of nature: "The octagon, by approximating the circle, encloses more space in its walls than the square, besides being more compact and available."

Bird named his home Woodchester Villa after his birthplace in England. When residents of Bracebridge commented on the unusual design of his residence, he explained he wanted to build "a bird cage to keep my Birds in."

Woodchester Villa, overlooking the Muskoka River on the north, was truly a classic structure. John Rempel in his book *Building with Wood* says that Woodchester Villa is one of the largest houses of the octagonal style in Ontario. "It has so many features of Fowler's octagonal plan that it could be considered the classic example in Ontario."

The Bird woollen mill operated until 1954, when it was closed because the prospects for markets were so poor that production ceased. Today, Woodchester Villa is a museum operated by the Bracebridge Historical Society and was first opened to the public on June 22, 1980.

Near to Bracebridge are Port Carling and Port Sandfield. In 1860 Vernon Bayley Wadsworth, a survey student, was part of a crew mapping the Muskokas. Vernon shared some observations: "The Indian Village of Obogawanung, now Port Carling, consisted of some 20 log huts, beautifully situated on the Indian River and Silver Lake with a good deal of cleared land about it used as garden plots, and the Indians grew potatoes, Indian corn, and other vegetable products. They had no domestic animals but dogs and no boats but numerous birch canoes.

"I feel sure Lake Muskoka was named after a Medicine Man of ObogawanungVillage, although other residents of that section say that it was named after an Indian from Lake Simcoe. Lake Rosseau, in my opinion, was named after an Indian interpreter named Rosseau who was employed by Governor Simcoe in his treaties and interviews with Indian tribes on Lake Ontario and with the Indians of Georgian Bay and Lake Simcoe districts."

Wadsworth adds, "William King and his Band at Port Carling were removed by orders of the Indian Department from their Village there to the reserve at Parry Island. I inquired of him why Skeleton Lake was so named. He stated that they called it Spirit Lake (Paukuk Lake) for the reason that ghosts and spirits were there."

Huntsville

The town of Huntsville is situated on the Muskoka River, 40 kilometres (25 miles) north of Bracebridge, and it derives its name from Captain George Hunt, who was the first permanent settler of the village. Hunt arrived here with his wife and family in 1869. He was responsible for the Muskoka Road reaching farther north to Huntsville and for the bridge being built across the river. Huntsville's first church services and school classes were held in his log cabin. In 1870 a post office opened, with Hunt as postmaster. He was a man with temperance principles and he made it a condition on the deeds, issued on his original acreage, that no intoxicating liquor was to be sold on the premises.

Construction of the locks on the Muskoka River between Mary Lake and Fairy Lake in 1877 augmented the growth of this settlement. The same year the steamer *Northern* was launched at Port Sydney. Travellers could now get from Bracebridge via Utterson to Port Sydney by stage, then by steamer to Huntsville, Fairy Lake, and Lake Vernon. Two years later Huntsville had two hotels, five general stores, a hardware store, a butcher, shoemaker, tailor, two blacksmiths, seven carpenters, a pump and wagon shop, and two sawmills.

Huntsville was incorporated as a village in 1886, with a population of 400 residents. The same year, the Northern Railway reached the village and the lumber industry began to flourish with shipping potential increased. Several sawmills were built, including those of the Whaley Lumber Company and the Whiteside Lumber Company. Fred Francis and Duncan McCaffery erected planing mills, and a gristmill and a woollen mill were also built. Ten trains a day connected to the lake steamers. Promotional books encouraging tourism also appeared, books such as the *Muskoka and Northern Lakes* publication.

Seven years after the firey tragedy at Gravenhurst, the community of Huntsville experienced its own firey blaze on April 18, 1894. What started out as a spring cleanup resulted in a loss of 75 percent of the business sector. At 10 past noon, a blaze travelled, without discrimination, on both sides of Main Street. The fire was fanned by a stiff southeast wind and spread so quickly that people were powerless to stop it. Many residents took to boats in the river to escape the orange-black haze that hung above the community.

The steamer *Excelsior* was moored at the wharf when the fire broke out. George Hutcheson and his son thought the ship was a good place to store what they could salvage from their burning store. A thousand dollars worth of goods were placed on the lower deck, but, unable to steam up in time, the ship did not escape the flames. The *Excelsior* became a towering inferno, and all that was left was a charred hull. Hutcheson remarked, "It was a burning furnace with all of my goods on it. We cut it loose during all the excitement, hoping to save the boat and my things, but the craft was taken up by the current and sucked into the sheet of fire."

In the meantime, four firemen from Bracebridge and Gravenhurst had been locked up. Apparently, the firemen were intoxicated with liquor, singing dirty songs and cussing. Their cohorts threatened to destroy the jail if they were not released, and so they were, indeed, released from jail. The whole town suffered losses, but nevertheless, they rebuilt and eventually regained their former prosperity.

In the late 19th and early 20th centuries, Huntsville developed into a tourist resort as steamer cruises became more popular. The Hanna and Hutcheson Brothers established a factory to produce flooring, broom handles, and other products. In 1902 they organized the Muskoka Wood Manufacturing Company and built a mill and flooring factory which produced the well-known "Red Deer" brand flooring.

In 1891 the Huntsville Tannery was established. It was certainly a large operation, with a weekly output from 1,200 to 1,600 dressed hides, averaging 9 kilograms (20 pounds) each. The hides were imported to the United States, and the hemlock bark used in the tanning process reached 6,000 to 7,000 cords per annum, which, at five dollars a cord, represented $30,000 to $35,000. Sawmills monopolized every navigable lake and stream in the district.

In 1920 C.O. Shaw opened the Bigwin Inn, which soon became a popular summer resort. Other inns and campgrounds also began to appear in the area. Tourists flocked to the Muskokas, and Huntsville was a prized attraction. The development of ski resorts gave them a year-round clientele and a busier-than-most downtown.

Muskoka is indeed a special place. No wonder the Natives admired and respected it so. Tradition abounds in every nook and cranny of this district, and the people who live here can be quite protective of it. Concern and caution are the two words often spoken today. Many people worry about future development and the impact it will have on the water and on the wildlife. The existence of parks like Algonquin and the maintenance of crown lands is essential to the protection of this natural splendour — the guarantee that this magnet of nature will continue to pull at people.

North Bay

North Bay is a vibrant city of 54,000 people, nestled between Lake Nipissing and Trout Lake. From its beginnings North Bay has been a centre of transportation. The first business in the area was carried out by canoe, and the fact that North Bay was on a system of interconnected waterways was significant during the fur-trading days. These waters provided the fastest route from Montreal through the Great Lakes and beyond.

In 1961 a new set of children's swings for Champlain Park became the key to a major discovery of artifacts from the past. The site was immediately registered as the La Vase North Bank Archaeological Site. In August 1995 excavations of the area began as part of the Heritage North Project. In May and June 1996, Laurentian University conducted an archaeological field school that located burnt timbers and other evidence, which identified the site as the location of Fort Laronde, an historic fur-trading post.

Fort Laronde was established in the late 1700s, or early 1800s, by Eustache de Laronde, an independent Metis fur trader associated with the Northwest Company of Montreal. In 1821 the post was closed and moved to Garden Island near the Sturgeon River as a result of the merger of the Northwest Company and the Hudson's Bay Company.

The North Bay region was the site of several such trading posts prior to the arrival of the Canadian Pacific Railway in 1882. John McIntyre Ferguson, nephew of the vice-president of the CPR, had visited the area and settled here, a year before the railway.

Archives of Ontario

North Bay, V.E. Day, 1945. One of the many V.E. Day celebrations that occurred all over Ontario.

Only a log cabin occupied the site when the CPR laid a new section of line at "the great, north bay" of Lake Nipissing. John Ferguson purchased property and played a substantial role in the development of the settlement. It was Ferguson who unintentionally gave the place its name, when he directed a shipment of building materials from Pembroke to be sent to him at the "north bay." Ferguson served as postmaster in 1881–82, and later as mayor from 1919–22.

North Bay became a railway community with business enterprises surrounding the railway yards, including a roundhouse, coal depot, a repair station, and a few dwellings.

Jim Mulligan owned the first stores in North Bay, J.W. Richards established a tinsmithy in 1885, and John Bourke operated a steam-powered sawmill at the west end of the settlement. The following year he used his steam generator to supply a portion of North Bay with electricity.

The railway brought with it a surge of settlers and workers and, by 1890, North Bay was incorporated as a town. The community became the judicial seat of the Nipissing District in 1895.

In 1905 North Bay became the southern terminus of the Timiskaming and Northern Ontario Railway (Ontario Northland Railway). A gateway to the rich resources of the north, it had access to primary resources such as nickel, iron, copper, gold, platinum, silver, and cobalt, all of which assisted in the growth of North Bay. Rail connection soon included an extension of the Grand Trunk Railway from Gravenhurst to Lake Nipissing, and North Bay became a major distribution centre and link between northern resources and markets south.

The 1930s in North America were depression years, in every sense of the word. Money markets collapsed and crops failed; people were poor, then hungry, and after years of this, utterly without hope.

The whole continent was in the grip of a terrible malaise, and its people looked for heroes and a better tomorrow. This was the age of Shirley Temple, Charles Lindbergh, Fred Astaire, and Ginger Rogers — and the Dionne quintuplets.

So much has been written about the Dionne quintuplets, including Pierre Berton's excellent book, *The Dionne Years*. There have been movies made, and a few years ago they were in the news again, but for less positive reasons.

It all began on May 28, 1934, at about 1:00 a.m., when Elzire Dionne, the 25-year-old mother of six, told her husband, Oliva, that she wanted assistance for the delivery of her seventh baby. Two local midwives arrived and then they sent for Dr. Dafoe. The first baby was born at 4:00 a.m. By the time Dr. Dafoe had arrived, there were two. And they kept coming.

Conditions in a big city hospital at the time would have been rudimentary for such an event, compared to modern technology; here, in Corbeil, in 1934, in the Dionne's humble farmhouse, they were woefully inadequate. Still, Canadian resourcefulness came into play. A basket was set on two chairs in front of the open oven. An eyedropper was used to give the babies warm water. Minute amounts of rum were administered every day.

Their combined weight at birth was only 13 pounds, 3 ounces. Each perfectly formed, identical baby girl weighed approximately 2.2 pounds (about one kilogram). Yvonne, Annette, Cecile, Emilie, and Marie spent the first month of their lives in an incubator; miracle upon miracle, they survived. The Dionne family, and North Bay, would never be the same again.

As soon as the news was out, the Dionne family was grist for the media mill. Promoters from all over North America saw a huge opportunity and felt that a simple French-speaking family might be easy prey. By the time the "quints" were two months old, the Ontario government had made them wards of the Province, and by the time they were four months old, they were removed from their parents' home.

"Quintland" was close to the Dionne homestead, but the Dionne parents soon had to make an appointment to see their daughters. The other siblings were denied access because Dr. Dafoe felt that children were "germ carriers." The quintuplets had become a five-child industry.

Buildings popped up around Quintland, including souvenir stands that were operated by Oliva Dionne, with a sign that said SOUVENIRS — REFRESHMENTS, OPERATED BY PARENTS OF THE WORLD'S MOST FAMOUS BABIES. There was a nursery, a staff house, a playground building where the public could observe the quints, and an observation gallery. These children were raised in a goldfish bowl. Visitors entered the gallery in groups of 100 and viewed the children through mesh-covered windows. The compound was surrounded by mesh fencing, and police were in charge of crowd control; 3,000,000 people visited, and the line of cars sometimes stretched for 4 kilometres (2.5 miles).

So-called fertility stones lined the path to the observation platform and were free to visitors. Each morning the Ontario Department of Highways replenished the supply of stones from the shores of Lake Nipissing. Everyone needs to believe in miracles, and it appeared that the Department of Highways did, too!

The image of the girls graced, among other things, lunch boxes, serving trays, and china, and they figured prominently in print — notably, ad campaigns for all manner of food and other products, including General Motors and McCormick's Biscuits. Dr. Dafoe ran the complex, and he and the other guardians appointed by the government determined the girls' fate.

The town of North Bay saw the end of the bitter depression. Tourism meant prosperity to anyone who could provide accommodation, food, or souvenirs. By 1939 $2,500,000 had been spent in North Bay by those eager to see the Dionne quintuplets.

This did not come to an end until the girls were almost 10 years old! They were finally reunited with their parents, and together they moved to a new home, but with less than satisfactory results. Isolated and controlled from their earliest memory, they and their family had difficulty adjusting to a normal life together.

Emilie died in 1954, during an epileptic seizure. In 1970 Marie was found dead in her apartment; she had suffered from depression and other health problems. The surviving Dionnes publicly approached the Ontario government in the mid-1990s for a portion of the money they had earned during the 1930s. After some public pressure, the government agreed to award them $2,800,000.

Eventually, Stan Guignard, a former Canadian heavyweight boxing champion, took over the Dionne homestead. Guignard had the house moved to North Bay, where it stands today as a museum. Visitors can tour the rooms the Dionnes lived in and browse through original artifacts and paintings.

The quintets are probably North Bay's most unusual and famous story, but it is only one story from the area. North Bay is now a major city with many government offices, a major cruise ship, Nipissing University, and Canadore College; the Northwest Trading Company has been gone since 2008. Change is ever-present, ongoing, and what we think we know today is history by tomorrow.

Oshawa

The land now occupied by Oshawa was once covered by dense forest. A broad stream, the Oshawa Creek, found its way to Lake Ontario. Those who originally traversed these waters were the Natives called the Mississaugas. They lived in a large settlement where Port Perry now stands.

In the spring the Natives bundled their pelts and paddled to a spot called Oshawa harbour. Once there, they headed west to a French trading post at the mouth of the Credit River.

The French established a trading post in the Oshawa harbour in 1750 called *Cabane de Plombe*, meaning "lead or shot house," near the mouth of the Oshawa Creek. Nine years later they abandoned their log structure. It remained empty until 1794, when a party of six white settlers arrived in the area and sought refuge there. They were Benjamin Wilson, his wife, and his two sons, James and David, as well as two young men, L. Lockwood and E. Ransome. The Wilson family built a frame house on high ground about 136 metres (150 yards) back from the lakeshore. Here, Nancy Wilson came into the world, the first white child born in the Oshawa district.

On October 15, 1792, Roger Conant landed on Canadian soil at Newark (now Niagara-on-the-Lake) after crossing the Niagara River on a flat-bottomed scow ferry. He journeyed eastward along the north shore of Lake Ontario until he arrived in Darlington, where he hastily erected a log dwelling on his 1,200 acres before the winter set in. Four years later he brought his family from the United States to settle on this property. To invest the $5,000 in gold he had brought with him, he engaged in the fur trade. He had three flat-bottomed, broad-beamed Durham boats built in Montreal, which he promptly filled with blankets, traps, knives, guns, flints, ammunition, and beads to trade with the Natives for furs. He quickly accumulated a considerable fortune, which he invested in holdings of land along the north shore of Lake Ontario.

Conant, obviously a colourful character, once remarked that the salmon were so plentiful in those days that while he was paddling his canoe, the salmon raised his canoe up in the water. Conant went into the packing business and shipped some of those plentiful salmon by the barrel to the United States, at an excellent price. From the proceeds of one of these ventures, he bought yet another 150-acre farm on the shore of Lake Ontario. In 1811 he left his log cabin to build a frame house near the Oshawa harbour. Little did he know that his home would play a part in the War of 1812, just one year later.

When General Hull surrendered his whole command of 2,500 men at Detroit, on August 15, 1812, a serious question arose: what would the British do with so many prisoners? The redcoats decided to send the American prisoners to Quebec. Unable to furnish enough boats, many prisoners were forced to walk along the shore of Lake Ontario. The prisoners and guards alike were fed at various places along the route. When they arrived at Roger Conant's home without warning, the family quickly set a large pot of potatoes on the fire to boil. A churning of butter had been done that day and a ham had been boiled the preceding day. The guards were outnumbered two to one, but no one escaped while feasting at this house.

A few days before Roger Conant died in 1821, he did a very odd thing. Conant decided to bury his gold in a large iron bake kettle on the bank of the Oshawa Creek. When it was noticed that the kettle was missing, a search began but failed to reveal its whereabouts. Many have attempted to find this buried treasure, but, alas, without success.

Around 1800, William and Moody Farewell and Jabez Lynde arrived in the area. Moody Farewell built a saw and gristmill on Harmony Creek and a tavern on Dundas Street. When regular stage traffic travelled this route, the Farewell tavern became a popular resting place. Jabez Lynde was the first pioneer to own property in what later became the village of Oshawa.

During this time several small communities were scattered about the area, clustered around the mills at the edges of the many creeks. On Dundas Street Edward Skae operated a store, and the settlement that grew around it became known as Skae's Corners. Other early settlers of Oshawa included the Annis, Henry, Ritson, Ross, and McGill families.

In 1840 the settlers of Skae's Corners petitioned the government to establish a post office. At a meeting Sydenham was the name chosen by the citizens, until Moody Farewell arrived with two Native companions. The two Natives were asked to suggest a name and they offered *Oshawa*, the translation of which is said to be "crossing between the waters" or "where the canoe is exchanged for the trail."

Oshawa received official village status in 1850, with a population of about 1,000. Three years later Oshawa became a customs port. In 1856 the Grand Trunk Railway was completed from Toronto to Montreal, passing to the south of Oshawa.

The new rail and harbour facilities helped to promote industrial growth in the area. A.S. Whiting had the distinction of being the first industrialist in Oshawa, establishing the Oshawa Manufacturing Company, producing agricultural implements in 1852. Whiting originally started out as a clock salesman in 1842. His methods of operation, as he related them himself, are on record. He would bring 100 clocks, from the factory in New England, by boat to Port Hope. There he would buy a team of horses and a spring wagon, and with the clocks on board, start out on a selling tour in the surrounding district. At a farm house, he would set up a clock in the kitchen. He would then depart, leaving the clock, which he said he would collect later on his return trip. It was quite a successful technique: he very seldom had to take a clock back!

George H. Pedlar established the next plant, a tin and sheet metal business, in 1861. The new rail and harbour facilities attracted many businessmen to Oshawa, including Robert McLaughlin. The McLaughlin family was to have a profound influence on the development of the community.

Robert McLaughlin manufactured carriages in the hamlet of Enniskillen, northeast of Oshawa. In 1876 he bought a lot in Oshawa and there he erected a modest three-storey building with a separate blacksmith shop constructed of brick. He sold the balance of the lot to the town, where a jail was built and later the city hall.

In 1879 Oshawa was incorporated as a town. By 1894 the town had an electric street railway with nine miles of main track and three miles of second track. On December 7, 1899, the McLaughlin Carriage Company buildings burned to the ground. Robert's son, Robert S. McLaughlin, who was by then a partner in the company, was reported to have said, "We could only stand and watch our life's work go up in flames, not only we McLaughlins, but the 600 men who depended for a living on the carriage works."

The town of Oshawa felt a loyalty to the McLaughlin family and offered a loan of $50,000 to be repaid as was convenient. It was a good thing, too, because the city of Belleville had contacted the McLaughlins, while the ruins were still smouldering, to offer them a bond issue and a big cash bonus if they would rebuild their factories in Belleville. The McLaughlins chose to remain in Oshawa.

By 1900 the McLaughlin Carriage Company was back in business. In the United States, in 1905, the automobile emerged from the horseless-carriage stage and became an industry. The Buick Motor Company, now two years old, had just been taken over by a carriage builder named William C. Durant.

R.S. McLaughlin was determined to persuade his brother George that automobiles had a place in the world. He travelled to the United States to learn more about what was being done in the automobile field. There he met with Durant, then returned to Toronto, purchased a Model F two-cyclinder Buick, and drove it home to Oshawa. Before he was halfway there, he knew that this was the car he wanted to make in Canada. R.S. sat down and talked to his family. He waited for his father to contemplate this new idea, wondering if the response would be to continue to build carriages. Instead, his father told him to go ahead, if he thought he could make it work. That was all he needed to hear, and before the dust could settle, the McLaughlins were busy designing their first car, right down to the beautiful brass McLaughlin radiator. Those were the beginnings of the car company that was to become General Motors of Canada.

Author's collection

Oshawa, 1941. When gasoline was rationed, Sam McLaughlin set a gas-saving example by returning to the hay-fuelled McLaughlin carriage.

The McLaughlins had obtained the rights to manufacture Chevrolet cars and formed the Chevrolet Motor Car Company of Canada in 1915. In 1918 the McLaughlin Motor Car Company of Canada was purchased by General Motors and incorporated as General Motors of Canada Limited, with R.S. McLaughlin as president.

Oshawa annexed part of East Whitby Township in 1922 and became an incorporated city two years later. A further annexation of part of the township took place in 1951. Two World Wars stimulated the expansion of Oshawa's industries, and although the depression of the 1930s cancelled some of the growth, recovery was rapid.

It was during the Second World War that Oshawa became the site of a secret intelligence organization. In 1940 Sir William Stephenson, the founder of British Security Co-ordination, was sent to the United States by the British prime minister, Winston Churchill, to establish an intelligence network that would eventually encompass all of the western hemisphere. One of the initial Canadian projects was to purchase land in Oshawa and supervise the construction of buildings for a training centre. The place was known locally as Camp X, by the Canadian government as file 25-1-1, and by the British government as STS 103.

Camp X was the first secret agent training school in North America. It was designed to help the Americans and Canadians learn the art of espionage. For that reason it was built where easy access to the United States was possible: on the shores of Lake Ontario.

Camp X opened its doors to recruits just two days after the bombing of Pearl Harbor. During the war years, Canada, the United States, and Britain trained secret agents in the art of clandestine warfare. Due to the extreme secrecy surrounding the 275-acre site, local residents of Whitby and Oshawa were unaware of these activities. Some local residents worked at the Camp, but they were sworn to secrecy.

One of the intelligence officers who attended the camp was Ian Fleming, and he is believed to have conceived the idea for his series of James Bond novels while stationed at the camp. Major Paul Dehn, a poet, musician, and lyricist, who was chief instructor at Camp X, used his talents to write propaganda. From his wartime experience he went on the write the screenplays of such famous films as *The Spy Who Came in from the Cold*. The "Shanghai Buster," William Ewart Fairbairn, invented the famous double-edged commando knife and taught Camp X recruits the art of silent killing. The 1976 international bestseller about Stephenson, *A Man Called Intrepid*, claimed that Camp X represented "the clenched fist" of all Allied secret operations in the Second World War.

The camp closed in 1946 and remained vacant for several years. All that remains is a small park by Lake Ontario, off Thickson Road, beside the Liquor Control Board of Ontario warehouse. The park is simply named Intrepid Park. In front of it is a short curving wall moulded in grey concrete and mounted with four flagpoles. Embedded in the wall is a bronze plaque.

Today, in 2011, Oshawa remains the home of General Motors of Canada. This company greatly assists in growing many smaller, related industries, who find a ready market in the GM corporation. The question arises, however, "How much longer will they last with gas and other energy crises?"

The cultural centre of the city is represented by three museums: the Henry House and the Robinson House museum are located at the bottom of Simcoe Street by Lake Ontario. The Canadian Automotive Museum is found on Simcoe Street near the downtown district. The Robert McLaughlin Gallery, situated next to city hall, represents the work of many well-known Canadian artists. Visitors to the city may also enjoy the recreational activities included in the more than 50 parks. Windfield Farms, Canada's National Stud Farm, lies north of the city, as does Durham College of Applied Arts and Technology.

Oshawa's main historic site, Parkwood, the estate of the late Colonel R.S. McLaughlin, stands on Simcoe Street next to the Oshawa General Hospital. Sightseers can tour this formidable mansion and view the magnificent landscape and expansive grounds.

R.S. McLaughlin had this to say about life: "The things I cherish are harder-wearing than gold, the worth of a lifetime spent working at a job that drew the best from me and the men I worked beside. Above all these, I treasure the love of my wife and the affection of my family. Those are the things of real worth in my life."

Ottawa

W ho could have imagined that this raw frontier town, situated on the south bank of the Ottawa River, would one day become the capital of a new country.

In the spring of 1826, Colonel By was ordered to oversee the construction of the Rideau Canal. This artificial waterway was designed to link the Ottawa River with Lake Ontario to provide an alternative strategic route between Upper and Lower Canada.

Colonel By quickly established his base of operations at the present site of Hull, Quebec, near the headlocks of this canal. Phileman Wright, an American, arrived at this site in 1800, with his wife and a few other settlers. Wright eventually established a gristmill, a tannery, a blacksmith shop, and a bakery, and the community became known as Wright's town or Wrightville, until 1875, when it changed to Hull.

It was the governor-in-chief's wife, Lady Dalhousie, who lifted the first shovel of earth of this 200-kilometre-long (125 mile) canal project. News of this massive canal project attracted hundreds of Irish labourers from the cities of Montreal and Quebec. Although work was plentiful, housing shortages abounded. Hazardous working conditions meant there were numerous injuries and deaths from explosions, falling rocks, and trees.

In 1827 Colonel By turned his attention to establishing a townsite at the canal's northern terminus, where some of the early settlers had put down roots. This new settlement was named Bytown, in his honour.

Jehiel Collins, a United Empire Loyalist, was actually the first to settle on the present-day site of Ottawa. He arrived in 1809 at a canoe landing on the south bank of the river below the Chaudiere Falls. In 1817 a civil engineer named John Burrows settled on 200 acres that is now the downtown core of Ottawa. The property was bounded in the north by present-day Wellington and Rideau Streets, on the south by Laurier Avenue, on the west by Bronson Avenue, and on the east by Waller Street. Burrows sold his property to Nicholas Sparks for the sum of 95 pounds.

When Sparks heard about the proposed Rideau Canal, he saw potential! Land meant money, and he quickly surveyed his own property and sold lots. He even designated a new street to be named after him. His wealth and generosity soon gained Sparks a tremendous influence in the political arena and the social circles of Bytown. He donated land for the first Methodist chapel, the Anglican Church, the courthouse, and the gaol. Bytown's first town hall was situated on land owned by Sparks.

The early days of Bytown prompted building — houses, shops, stores and, of course, taverns. An outbreak of swamp fever in 1828 greatly reduced the pioneer population of French, Irish, Scottish, English, and American settlers. Work in Bytown ground to a halt. The first civilian cemetery appeared on land between the present Metcalfe and Elgin Streets. Anglicans, Presbyterians, and Roman Catholics were placed in separate burial sections. Life was so grim that the Royal Sappers and Miners, a contingent of soldier-labourers from England, deserted the fever-stricken settlement. Many Bytown workers turned to alcohol to ease their anxiety. Since law and order was yet to be established, street fights became a daily occurrence. No one was safe! The swamp fever epidemic eventually subsided, and by 1832, the Rideau Canal had been completed. Bytown began, once again, to flourish, this time as a lumber centre.

Colonel By, in the meantime, who had actualized the wishes of his superior British officers, was summoned to England. Perhaps he was to be commended or promoted for his loyal service. No one ever dreamed it would be to stand accused, by a parliamentary committee, of the misuse of funds.

Although Colonel By was exonerated, his spirit was broken. He never returned to Bytown. He was the man who saw the true potential of this place, the man once quoted as saying, "This land will be very valuable some day. It will be the capital of this country." Colonel By died a very disillusioned man, on February 1, 1836, at the age of 53.

Rideau Falls, Ottawa, in the 1880s. Small wonder Colonel By understood the value of this land.

By the 1850s Bytown was linked by rail to other larger centres and had become a community of new opportunities. In 1855 the town became a city and was renamed Ottawa. The population was nearing 10,000.

When the union of Upper and Lower Canada occurred in 1841, cities such as Quebec, Montreal, York, and Kingston had vied to be the capital. Kingston managed to be appointed as the capital for a short time, as did Montreal. Government officials then believed it was beneficial to alternate the seat of government every four years. The need for permanency became apparent, however, and in 1857 Queen Victoria was asked to choose the city that would become the long-serving capital.

Sir Richard William Scott, Ottawa's member of Parliament, prepared an eloquent summation which cited the advantages of his city's rail and water communication as well as its central geographical location to Canada East and Canada West by way of Union Bridge across the Ottawa River. On December 31, 1857, the Queen's notice was contained in a letter from the desk of the colonial secretary. It read in part: "I am commanded by the Queen to inform you, that in the judgement of Her

Majesty, the City of Ottawa combines more advantages than any other place in Canada for the permanent seat of the future government of Province." A year later, in 1858, Ottawa became the capital of Canada.

Politicians needed to think about designing a building to house the seat of government in this new capital. On May 21, 1859, the *Ottawa Tribune* posted "Notice to Architects" specifying the budget for the buildings: "For Parliament House, $300,000; for Departmental Building $240,000." The site chosen for the Parliament buildings was Barracks Hill, deemed the most desirable location, overlooking the Ottawa River.

The first sod was turned on December 20, 1859. The Centre Block took six years to complete. Delays followed one after the other due to instability in the underlying rock bed, the need to install water tanks in case of fire, and the transportation of the stone from the Nepean quarry, 12 miles away.

On September 1, 1860, the Prince of Wales (later King Edward VII) laid the cornerstone of the original Centre Block of the Gothic-style Parliament buildings, comprised of three copper-roofed stone structures: the East Block, the West Block, and the Centre Block.

Architecturally, the Parliament buildings represented Canada's best example of the developed, picturesque Gothic revival style. Features borrowed from medieval architecture included pointed arches, lancet windows with tracery, pinnacles with crockets, prominent exposed buttresses, and contrasting, variegated stonework, set off by brick trim. The Centre Block was first designed in 1859, reworked in 1863, and completed in 1866.

Disaster struck parliament hill on February 3, 1916, while the House of Commons was in session. Fire broke out and the Centre Block was gutted. The entire incident remains a mystery. The East and West Blocks and library were untouched. The Canadian poet, Duncan Campbell Scott, was witness to it all. "The fire was terrible and tragic; it was the most terrifying and beautiful sight I have ever seen ... I hope that the building may be restored without the practice of any vandalism, but I have my doubts. I hear talk of 'a larger, more imposing, up-to-date building.' The very phrases make one shudder. We had a building that was beautiful and harmonized with the site, and there will be some people who will want to destroy it because they can put up something more beautiful.

Picture of the corner of Rideau and Sussex Streets in 1865.

If they can put up a more beautiful building, let them put it somewhere else. Let us preserve the beauty that we have."

The damage was, as it turned out, too great and the building had to be demolished. For the interim, the government relocated to the Victoria Memorial Museum (now the Museum of Nature) at the foot of Metcalfe Street. Architect John A. Pearson's Neo-Gothic design won the architectural competition, and the Centre Block was erected between 1916 and 1920. The new structure contained 490 rooms, including the House of Commons and the Senate Chamber. In 1919 the Prince of Wales laid the cornerstone of the Peace Tower, a majestic structure rising to a height of 88 metres (291 feet). With 53 bells that range in weight from five to 10,000 kilograms (10 to 22,400 pounds), the Peace Tower remains one of the world's finest carillons.

In 1868 a distinct stone mansion was constructed by a prominent businessman named Joseph Merrill Currier. He chose a site overlooking Governor's Bay and christened it Gorphwysfa (the Welsh word for "place of peace"). The property was later owned by lumber barons until the government of Canada expropriated the property in 1946 to be the official residence for the Prime Minister. Today, we know the house as 24 Sussex Drive.

Visitors to Ottawa cannot help but walk by or through the Chateau Laurier Hotel. This impressive building on Rideau Street was started in 1908 and finished in 1912 by architects Ross and MacFarlane. The design they chose was a chateau-style, which had become popular for railway hotels across Canada. As you enter the hotel, your first view is of the ornately carved wooden panelling in the front foyer. In 1911 tourist-guide comments included: "The corridors are divided into sections by means of fire doors to separate them in an emergency, although the hotel is absolutely fireproof, no wood, except frames for doors and baseboards, being used in its construction. The main corridors lead directly to fire escapes, iron balconies and stairways inside the building. All the windows and service floors will be screened with the best Canadian-made fly screens, and a special refrigerating room will be provided to freeze the garbage until it is removed from the building."

It was Boston-born Bradford Lee Gilbert who won the design competition for the Chateau Laurier. Gilbert, for no known reason, was fired in 1908. Although his design had met with Cabinet approval a year earlier, the Montreal firm of Ross and MacFarlane replaced Gilbert.

The architectural design of the building also included an underground tunnel linking the railway hotel to Union Station, built in 1912, and now housing the Government Conference Centre. Many people at the time expressed concern for safety in an underground tunnel. People felt this tunnel might attract "not only pickpockets but gentlemen whose misdemeanours were of a far more serious nature." Speculation still exists that tunnels were also built to Parliament Hill.

Looking at the building from the street level, you can see sheer sandstone walls reaching up to the top floors. The steeply pitched copper roofline is a dramatic feature. The castle-like atmosphere is enhanced by the corners, small towers that sport narrow slit windows as if for medieval archers.

The federal government remains the city's largest employer and tourism is the second-largest source of income in the city. Visitors remember Ottawa for the millions of tulips in the spring and for the world's longest skating rink, the Rideau Canal.

Colonel By and Queen Victoria could not have envisioned a more congenial place.

Parry Sound

The gateway to the 30,000 islands, Parry Sound, is situated on a bay, called a "sound," in Georgian Bay, at the mouth of the Sequin River. The First Nations peoples called this sound *Wau-sak-au-sing*, meaning "Shining Lake." It was Captain Bayfield of the Royal Navy who first surveyed the district and prepared a nautical chart of its waters, between 1822 and 1825. The Captain named the area Parry Sound, after Sir William Edward Parry, the arctic explorer.

The timber rights in the district were first owned, in 1857, by James and William Gibson of York County. They erected a water-powered sawmill on the Sequin River. The mill quickly became the nucleus of a settlement. There was a boarding house, a blacksmith shop, a few tiny log shanties, and a store. Early residents included Joseph Rogerson, Thomas Caton, D.F. Macdonald, Thomas McGown, and Frank Strain.

The actual founder of the town of Parry Sound was William Beatty. He arrived here from Thorold in 1863 with his father, William Sr., and his brother James. The Beatty family came in search of timber limits and fortuitously discovered that the Gibson timber rights were for sale. The Beatty property became known as the Parry Sound Estates. Their land consisted of the mill, several log cabins, and a 129.5-square-kilometre (50 mile) timber limit. Subsequently, they purchased an additional 2,000 acres of land at the mouth of the Sequin River. Today, this is Parry Sound.

Young William Beatty was enamoured of the rugged-shore country of Georgian Bay. His passion and love led to the development of a community. The land, where the business portion of the town stands,

Tom Sheridan's Boot and Shoe Shop on Sequin Street in 1908.

was cleared and laid out into village lots. The Beatty store, now the Beatty building, was constructed on the corner of James and Sequin Streets. Jim

Beatty, direct descendent, still operates from this site today.

From the beginning, William Beatty, affectionately known as "The Governor," took a strong stand against the legalization of liquor traffic in this settlement. He implemented the "Beatty Covenant"; this meant that all the deeds of land sold by him contained a clause stipulating that the holder of the land, whoever they may be, were liable to forfeit their title should liquor be sold on their premises. All such agreements were to remain legally binding for the lifetime of the parties signing, the lives of Queen Victoria's children, and 10 months after the deaths of the parties involved. It wasn't until 1950, after a plebiscite, that the restrictions were removed.

William Beatty was a well-educated man for his time, elected to the Senate of the University of Victoria in Cobourg, Ontario. William was a member of the Reform Party and a Wesleyan Methodist.

The Beatty brothers sold their mill and timber limits to Rathburn Company in 1871, and, only a few days later, Rathburn sold to A.G.P. Dodge and Company, who founded the Parry Sound Lumber Company.

While "Governor" Beatty worked to promote the well-being of his temperate settlement, another community was growing on the east shore of the inner harbour around a large mill built in 1873 by the Guelph Lumber Company. This settlement was called Carrington (later Parry Harbour) and posed a sharp contrast to Beatty's Parry Sound. This was a wet community. Mr. McGee erected the first tavern, a tavern which attracted many thirsty lumberjacks. Author Adrian Hayes, in his book *Parry Sound*, describes some of the hotels in Carrington:

> Taverns, by law, had to contain a minimum of four bedrooms with suitable bedding, beyond that required for the comfort of the tavern keeper and his family, and stabling facilities for at least six horses. There was to be both a dining room and a sufficiently stocked barroom to meet the needs of travellers. The Globe Hotel opened on November 19, 1874. This particular establishment flourished under a succession of owners, renovations and name changes. In its last incarnation it was the Queen's Hotel. The Thomson House, owned by Robert

Thomson opened for business during the summer of 1880. This was the first tavern on the site of the former Kipling Hotel, which burned on November 30, 1986. It wasn't until 1887, when a special Act of Parliament called for the union of the two settlements of Parry Sound and Parry Harbour, that the two were incorporated as the Town of Parry Sound.

The Beatty family were also involved in shipping on Georgian Bay. They owned a steamship business called the Beatty Lines and were pioneers in the Canadian shipping industry. Tragedy befell their shipping lines early one wintery day in 1879. The eerie and mysterious tragedy was also the last voyage of the steamer *Waubuno* and foretold by the last dream of a young bride of only three weeks.

The *Waubuno* was built by William Beatty in 1865 at Port Robinson. The hull was towed to Collingwood the same year and there the machinery was installed. The *Waubuno* was the beginning of fame for the Beatty ship lines on the upper lakes. The *Waubuno* was also the beginning of Canada Steamship Lines and Canadian Pacific Steamships.

For years the *Waubuno*, a 200-ton wooden sidewheeler, made weekly trips between Parry Sound and Collingwood, carrying freight and passengers during the flourishing shipping trade on Lake Huron and Georgian Bay. For the Beattys this lucrative business was heaven-sent, until a young bride of three weeks had a dream — a premonition of death.

On November 20, 1879, Mrs. Doupe, the new bride, and her husband, a doctor, retired for the night. They were to make their way from Collingwood to Parry Sound and from there to the village of McKeller, a few miles north in just two days time. There Dr. Doupe would take up the practice of medicine. That night, however, Mrs. Doupe saw the *Waubuno* beset with gigantic waves in her dreams. She and her husband, along with the other passengers, were struggling in the waters for their lives. She had foreseen her own death. Would they still board the ship?

The next day, news of her dream spread to the captain, the crew, and other passengers of the vessel. Although the story became a joke in Collingwood, many passengers opted not to sail in the face of this foreboding premonition.

Of that fateful day, David Williams, editor of the *Collingwood Enterprise Bulletin*, wrote, "Saturday, November 22nd, 1879, was a wild and winter-like day. The wind blew a gale and snow squalls were frequent. All the previous day it had been blowing great guns, and the *Waubuno* lay at the dock in Collingwood with one of the largest loads of the season, a number of passengers, a crew of 14, and all were waiting for the gale to abate sufficiently for her to start for Parry Sound."

Neither gale nor a bride's dream was going to stop Captain Burkett, master of the *Waubuno*, from setting sail. Besides, the Captain was eyeing the *Maganettawan*, a new ship put into service the same year by the Georgian Bay Lumber Company. It was lying across the harbor, loaded and ready to sail. The *Maganettawan* had beat the *Waubuno* on so many impromptu races along the North Shore that Captain Burkett was determined not to be out-sailed this time.

At 4:00 a.m. on November 22nd, the 150-foot steamboat silently sailed out of Collingwood without even a toot of its whistle to notify anyone of its departure. The gale, which had been blowing "great guns" for two days, had moderated. The trip to Parry Sound was short and relatively safe, normally, except for a 32-kilometre (20 mile) stretch between Hope Island and Lone Rock, where boats were exposed to open waters.

The bride and her husband had no chance to protest, since they were both asleep in their cabin when the *Waubuno* headed out. The ship was later sighted, on schedule, by John Hoar, the lightkeeper on Christian Island. At noon the *Waubuno* whistle was heard repeatedly by lumberjacks at Moon River. By then a heavy snowstorm was blowing, but no one thought anything of it. The ship often stopped for a whistle-pick-up of passengers among the islands. No one suspected that the *Waubuno* was in trouble. There was no reason to be anywhere near the Moon River, but rather safely in on the Waubuno Channel, north of Parry Island, and less than one hour away from her home port. What was she doing at the Moon River?

Apparently, when Captain Burkett came to the end of the northern leg of the course, at Lone Rock, he ran into a blinding snow storm and 64 kilometre- (40 mile) an-hour winds. Unable to obtain a clear sighting on Lone Rock, he dared not turn into the narrow western entrance of the Waubuno Channel.

At that point the Captain turned back and headed for the gap among the islands between Moose Deer Point and Copperhead. Although his navigation was on the nose, he had no way to know of an uncharted shoal in the middle of his projected passage. Normally, this shoal was 6 metres (20 feet) down, but the southwest gale changed all that. Seeing sprouting breakers here, the Captain dropped anchors, but the anchors did not catch. Years later, divers found a small anchor lying loose on the bottom and a larger anchor standing straight up, with five turns of anchor chain around the stock. The ship had shifted and come to rest when the main anchor chain caught a pinnacle of rock on the bottom and held. There, the *Waubuno* tossed in the breakers. It was only a question of time before something gave. Hence the distress signals. Suddenly, the foredeck gave way, the anchor was loose, and the ship was back in the gale. Downwind was an exposed rock called Burkett Rock. The paddlewheeler found it — hard. The engine-room machinery went to the bottom, the flotation hull ended up at Wreck Island, the ship split lengthwise, and everything else disappeared.

No survivors and no bodies were ever found. All of the life-preservers were later discovered among the wreckage, but no bodies. Why were the passengers not wearing life-preservers? What happened to the passengers? A mystery!

The tug *Mittie Grew* was sent out to search for the missing *Waubuno*. At the gap in the islands south of Copper Head, the tug saw evidence of a shipwreck. Wreckage lay scattered for miles, including a paddlewheel box and a lifeboat bearing the name of the *Waubuno*, but no bodies and no passengers. They had simply disappeared.

A short time later, several lawsuits were brought against the Beatty business. A special panel of experts in the courts presented such conflicting testimony that the court was unable to reach a decision on the case. It was concluded that the wreck was a great mystery, which would only be solved "when the sea gives up its dead."

The town of Parry Sound survived the blow. Passenger and freight steamers became numerous. These ships were admirably well-fitted and furnished for their service. In the South Channel between Parry Sound and Penetang, the sidewheeler *City of Toronto* ran daily trips. The *City of Parry Sound*, the *Northern Belle*, and the *Atlantic* called in

Archives of Ontario

Parry Sound, 1901: the Belvedere Hotel. Many grand hotels like this one were eventually lost to fire.

to Parry Sound on their semi-weekly trips. Steam yachts and tugs of the Parry Sound Yachting Fleet, as well as those of Galna & Danter, were present in force.

In 1888 the Districts of Muskoka and Parry Sound were formed into a United Provisional Judicial District and Parry Sound was named the District Town.

On January 21, 1926, the Georgian Bay Creamery Limited purchased River Street property and commenced operations in March of that year. The creamery closed down a few years ago, but the building had a few incarnations and is now Orr's.

At one time, Parry Sound hosted numerous tourist hotels. There was the Montgomery House owned by Joseph Calverly in 1881; this hotel served lumbermen and miners. The Canada Atlantic Hotel, operated by C.A. Phillips, had a beautifully appointed dining room. The Mansion House, on the corner of James and Mary Streets, was situated where the Brunswick Motor Hotel stands today. The Victoria House was on James Street, and just outside the town limits was Rose Point Hotel, owned by W.R. Thomson. There, guests enjoyed cruises on the Thomsons' steam yacht, the *Carlton*. And there was the Hotel Belvedere situated on the hill looking out over magnificent sunsets on Georgian Bay. It was a three-storey structure with double verandas. Fire took this glorious hotel down in the 1950s, and today it is the Belvedere Heights Home for the Aged.

Gone are all the grand hotels, the ships and the yachts. Some beautiful old homes remain. Industry has been kept at arm's length and the cultural life has found a niche of its own. There is The Festival of Sound (no pun intended) and Art in the Park. The surrounding townships have artists tucked away in every corner — inspired by this rugged land. The waterfront is beginning to develop, with two fine restaurants and an airplane service. The main street has potential but remains, as yet, undeveloped. The new four lanes of highway 400, north from Barrie, are begging for a new vision for this town. William Beatty had a dream and saw it come forth. What will the new dream be?

Pickering

In 1669 a French trader by the name of Pierre arrived at the Seneca village of Ganatsekwyagon, just east of the Rouge River in Scarborough. From there he set off across country to Lake Huron. In October of that year, Francois de Salignac de Fenelon, the first missionary to arrive in what is now Pickering Township, landed at Ganatsekwyagon.

Francois settled near the shore of Frenchman's Bay and opened a mission school. His first winter there was one of the worst winters on record. The frost penetrated so deeply that the ground remained frozen until June. As a result, Fenelon ministered to starving Natives at Frenchman's Bay. Food was so scarce, he was reduced to gnawing on the fungi that grew at the base of pine trees. Poor diet and rudimentary conditions led to the death of many women during childbirth. His main concern, at the time, was to prevent the Iroquois from placing live babies in the graves with their dead mothers. His attempts often failed, since few of the remaining women in the village were able or willing to care for the tiny orphans. The missionaries themselves attempted to care for the helpless infants, but were not often successful.

In 1791, surveyor Augustus Jones was authorized to survey the land between the Trent and Etobicoke Rivers and divide it into a series of townships. When Jones arrived to survey Pickering Township, he named Duffin's Creek, a stream of water flowing into Lake Ontario, after a trader by the same name. Although he seems to be somewhat of a myth, Duffin is said to have lived there. His cabin, it is said, was always open to travellers, one of whom found the door ajar, signs of a struggle, and blood on the floor. Duffin was gone and never seen again.

William Deak, another fur trader, settled at the mouth of Duffin's Creek in 1799. Between 1801 and 1807, a small group of houses formed a settlement at Duffin's Creek. In July 1807 David W. Smith, surveyor-general of Upper Canada (1792–1804), sold an 850-acre block around the creek to Timothy Rogers, a prominent Yonge Street Quaker. He began to build a sawmill and a gristmill near his house, southeast of the Kingston Road bridge, but four years later he was forced to sell his property and enterprises to settle his debts. He considered Pickering Township to be the centre of Quaker settlement in Upper Canada. Roger's grandchildren settled in both Pickering and Newmarket and pioneered the Imperial Oil Company development in Canada, as well as the Elias Rogers Coal Company. Although the Quaker population had increased the size of the settlement, it still only consisted of a few homes. By 1825 the population had reached 675.

During the early 1830s, Charles Fothergill, the noted naturalist, author, and politician, conceived an elaborate plan for a new community to be called Monodelphia. Churches, a tavern, a printing office, some mills, and a distillery were all part of his plan. Fothergill's plan failed, but his scheme brought further construction of homes and he himself lived there from 1831 to 1837.

In 1846 the population of Duffin's Creek was 130. There were now four churches, a grist-mill, a brewery, a tannery, several taverns, shoemakers, tailors, a blacksmith, and a wagon maker in the village. The excellent harbours, at both the mouth of the Rouge and at Frenchmen's Bay, were used for shipping, and Duffin's Creek was navigable for small boats as far up as the Kingston Road.

In 1856 the Grand Trunk Railway opened a line between Oshawa and Toronto. The railway benefitted the milling operations of the district. Each mill was served by a spur line of the Grand Trunk. By this time more than 50 percent of the township had been cleared of trees.

The U.S. Civil War in the 1860s hastened industrialization. War orders from the northern United States kept mills humming and encouraged farmers to put more land into wheat. Despite this, by the 1870s Pickering began to decline. Even at that time, many people could not afford to purchase Ontario farms and had headed west to homestead. The best pine and hardwood had already been exhausted and the remaining woodlots were cut again and again to pick up a little more ready cash. Many local flour mills ceased operation and were torn down or destroyed by fire.

Frenchman's Bay Harbour Company received a $70,000 grant in 1875 to improve the harbour. It was put to good use in the construction of a lighthouse, a wharf, and a 50,000-bushel grain elevator at the bay. The formation of a tiny village, with two hotels and numerous houses, evolved. Wagons often lined up on Liverpool Road to unload barley for breweries in the United States. Later, the imposition of duty on the barley closed off the market, and the harbour activity began to fade.

In 1881 the *Pickering News* described the village as a growing community and drew particular attention to Pickering Woodworks and other local industries and institutions. Pickering College, a residential secondary school built by the Quakers near their yearly meeting house at Pickering, was among those institutions. The college stood on five acres of beautiful grounds with a winding, tree-lined drive that lead up to the fine red-and-white brick structure that crowned the hill. Sectarian difficulties within the Society of Friends (Quakers) in Canada forced the closure of this Quaker-run school in 1885.

Pickering was incorporated as a village in March, 1953, and on January 1, 1974, it was amalgamated with the Town of Ajax to become Ajax-Pickering.

Today a walking tour of the quaint village of Pickering allows the visitor to step back in time. Beginning at the eastern edge of the village, a 19th century home, circa 1898, numbered 145 Kingston Road, has managed to survive the march of time; at 135 Kingston Rd. E. stands a typical Victorian house built circa 1887. South on Mill Street is the Friends Cemetery where 15 or more Quaker families, who had joined in Timothy Rogers settlement, were buried. Apparently Rogers, too, lies here in an unmarked grave. The Quaker Meeting House, built around 1867 at 117 Kingston Rd. E., is now the home of the Doric Lodge. It was built as the Canada Yearly Meeting House to serve Upper Canada. The first session took place on June 28, 1867. The stone regency cottage at 124 Kingston Rd. E. was built around 1850. The attractive two-storey frame house at 107 Kingston Rd. was built circa 1911 for Dr. Fields, a general practitioner in the village.

A good example of late Victorian architecture incorporating

polychromatic brickwork and Romanesque arched windows is a home, vintage 1870, at 97 Kingston Rd. E. Next door is a well-preserved red-frame cottage with an inviting entrance, built around 1842. This is one of the earliest houses in the village. Immediately opposite is a well-maintained Greek Revival white-frame house, built around 1880.

Turning north on Church Street and walking on the west side there is a white frame cottage, 22 Church Street N. This building was built circa 1880. A picturesque brick house with pointed gables at 68 Church Street south was built circa 1880. This home features a decorative front veranda with gingerbread and brackets. The spire of St. Francis de Sales Church (circa 1871), on Church Street S., was an early landmark in Pickering village.

North on Church and west on Randall Drive is St. George's Anglican Church, built circa 1841. This church was built of brick that was supplied by the Grand Trunk Railway in exchange for a railway right-of-way. Church lands extended at that time as far south as the present 401 highway.

At 22 Linton Road is one of the earliest properties in the village. This 1.5-storey Ontario cottage, built around 1843, was an adaption of the Regency style popular in Ontario from the early 19th century.

Winding through the back streets are a host of historic buildings. For example, 23 Elizabeth Street is an archetypal Gothic Revival cottage. And there is much more!

Far from the death and starvation of the first winter here, Ajax-Pickering is now almost a suburb of Toronto. As a matter of fact, there is continuous development from Toronto through Ajax-Pickering, and Whitby to Oshawa. Despite all of that growth, the historic village of Duffin's Creek remains visible.

Port Hope

The tall whispering pines in the Ganaraska Valley have always sounded a call of peace and tranquility for those who would stop to hear it.

The dense undergrowth on the hillsides provided abundant coverage for both rabbits and partridge. Deer and bear once roamed those forests in large numbers. It was here that a Mississauga tribe numbering 200 built their wigwams on the grassy slopes of the riverbank. They called their village Cochingomink. Like the Mississaugas, a fur trader named Peter Smith heard the call of this land and erected a log building in 1778.

Peter Smith's mission in life was to establish a trading-post business, and he did. His skill as a hunter and trapper won him great respect among the Mississaugas, which helped his endeavour to profit. In 1790 Smith decided it was time to leave. Another trapper, named Herchimere, took possession of Smith's cabin and kept the trading post going.

Unknown to Smith, his vision later spawned interest in the development of a community bearing his name. Only a year after his departure, the valley was surveyed, and the government offered grants of land to anyone willing to develop a settlement. Ironically, a United Empire Loyalist with the same surname, Elias Smith, and his friend Jonathan Walton, applied for settlement grants here.

On June 8, 1793, the soon-to-be fathers of Port Hope landed on the stony beach of their new home. This party of arrivals also included Myndert Harris, Lawrence Johnson, Nathaniel Ashford, James Stevens, and their families. By sunset a group of white tents dotted the flats across the creek from the trading post. By morning, construction of log houses, thatched with bark and with huge dutch fireplaces, had begun.

In no time at all, Smith and Walton helped to settle 40 families at a place later named Smith's Creek in honour of the first white settler, Peter Smith.

In 1817 Charles Fothergill received authority to establish a post office at Smith's Creek and was made postmaster. For some unknown reason, Fothergill was unimpressed by the name and proceeded to change it to Toronto. Two years later a petition was drawn up to request that the lieutenant governor of Upper Canada make the community a port of entry and clearance, where vessels from the United States could lawfully stop to discharge their cargoes. Inexplicably, this prompted the Executive Council of Upper Canada to require that the site be given yet another name. The inhabitants of the community met and G.S. Boulton suggested the name Port Hope in honour of Colonel Henry Hope, lieutenant governor of Quebec from 1785 to 1789. It was agreed. (It was 15 years later that the settlement of York adopted the name Toronto).

It was during these early years that some residents of Port Hope first encountered the "Haunted Meadow." This swampy spot had originally been created as the result of a beaver-dam. It was covered with a dense undergrowth and was surrounded by wild plum-trees in great profusion. The presence of "will-o'-the-wisps" gave it an uncanny reputation. According to Tony Diterlizzi and Holly Black, in their book entitled *Arthur Spiderwick's Field Guide to the Fantastical World Around You*, "The will-o'-the-wisps are spotted deep in forests, swamps, and other desolate places and appear as glowing orbs that move slowly over the landscape. These phantom lights are called by many different names. Elves particularly delight in using will-o'-the-wisps as a source of illumination and decoration for their revels.

"Lost travellers spotting wisps often believe they are seeing an artificial light and head toward it, causing them to become even more lost. Many have died, lost and alone, or fallen prey to some more dangerous faerie."

Early settlers steered clear of the Haunted Meadow. These feelings were magnified by the mysterious disappearance of an orphan-boy who was said to have been ill-treated and ultimately murdered by a surly old settler adjacent to the meadow. The boy, it was rumoured, had been buried in the meadow and his ghost was known to wander at night. This tale was supported by the accounts of two bold young men who, throwing caution to the wind, went to pick plums one evening at the so-called charmed circle. They had scarcely climbed into the trees when weird, guttural noises could be heard, and a ghostly figure began to flit around. They retreated hastily — with a gruesome story to tell everafter!

By the year 1826, the village had grown to include four general stores, a distillery, a tannery, three taverns, and one hotel. That year the first regular mail stage began to run through Port Hope. The coach stop was the old inn at the present site of the Queen's Hotel. In their heyday these stage coaches were large vehicles drawn by four horses, one of the picturesque elements that have rolled out of our sight today.

Commander John Tucker Williams established a 100-acre homestead in Port Hope in 1829. Williams named his house Penryn, after the village in England, where his parents were married in the late 1700s. In 1841 he ran for the Parliament of Upper Canada to represent the united counties of Durham and Northumberland. His campaign met with success, and one of his first acts as a member was to introduce the first copyright for published books in Canada. This bill was passed and became law. Mr. Williams held office until 1848, and in 1850 became the first mayor of Port Hope. He died four years later at the age of 65.

The railway arrived in 1856, when the Grand Trunk Line was opened between Montreal and Toronto via Port Hope. Thereafter, four passenger trains per day stopped at Port Hope.

One of the oldest private schools for boys in Canada, Trinity College School, relocated from the village of Weston to Port Hope, in 1868. The buildings were provided free of rent for three years. The reverend C.H. Badgley was then headmaster and was assisted by a staff of nine instructors. Known in some circles as the "Eton of Canada," it offered old-school traditions and associations, which rendered this nickname appropriate.

In 1870 Reverend Charles J.S. Bethune was appointed as the new headmaster. He was instrumental in creating a permanent institution. As a first step, in 1871, he purchased the 10 acres of land where the school still stands today. The central portion of the school was soon constructed. By an act of the Legislature of Ontario, passed during the session of 1871–72, Trinity College School was constituted a corporate

Library and Archives Canada

Port Hope's scenic main street circa 1880s.

body. The next year 96 boys attended there. That same year the Chapel and Dining Hall were completed. The following year the western wing of the old school was ready. The finished structure had a 90-metre (300 foot) southern face and extended 24 metres (80 feet) to the west, all at a cost of $62,000. In 1875 an additional 10 acres was purchased to ensure ample room for sports of all kinds.

Fire struck the school on April 27, 1893. It began about noon in the upper storey. Firemen, schoolboys, and townspeople fought the fire and successfully saved the building, but within a week another fire threatened to destroy the school. This fire was also extinguished before any serious damage happened. What are the odds that a fire would strike a third time in so short a time span? On Sunday morning, February 16, 1895, not quite two years later, the entire building was consumed by fire at a loss of $80,000.

School officials, with great faith in life and in tradition, set about to raise the money to rebuild. A new $90,000 structure was constructed on the same site as the old school. It was the same length as the original building but greater in breadth and height. Trinity College School still flourishes in Port Hope today.

Crime has given many communities notoriety. So too, Port Hope. On the morning of October 6, 1893, a crowd gathered outside the residence of Joseph Hooper. Three men emerged from the house. One was Chief of Police John Douglas, the second, Constable Jarvis, and the third was John Reginald Hooper, son of Joseph Hooper. John was handcuffed and escorted to a carriage. Despite his pallor John gave a military salute to the crowd with his free hand.

Two weeks earlier, sensational stories had begun to circulate regarding the death of his wife. She had apparently been taken off a CPR train at Terrebonne, Quebec, in a terrible condition and had died in the train station. Her husband had been travelling with her and returned to Port Hope on September 20th. He hurriedly buried his wife in the cemetery at Welcome.

John was well-known in town; he had been born in Port Hope and learned the trade of a printer in the newspaper office of the *Guide*. He subsequently served for some years in the military, "A" Battery, first in Kingston and then in Quebec. While in Quebec, he met and married a French-Canadian girl named Georgiana Leblanc. The couple went to live in Ottawa, where John entered the civil service in 1887 as a clerk in the Post Office Department. There was no record to indicate that his wife suffered from mental problems, yet on October 14, 1891, he committed her to the Rockwood Asylum in Kingston.

In the spring of 1893, John developed an interest in a young woman by the name of Alice Stapley. Unwilling to expose his true marital status, he posed as a widower. He even placed a fake notice of his wife's death in a newspaper in Quebec, which stated that she had died in Lille, France, but no date of death was given. A few weeks later he placed a second death notice in another newspaper, stating that she had died in Savannah, Florida. What did Hooper have in mind for his wife?

On September 10, 1893, he arrived in Kingston and removed his wife from the asylum. The reason he gave was that he was taking her back to her parents' home at St. Ambroise de Kildare, Quebec. During the journey, at Louiseville, Quebec, he removed her from the train and attempted to drown her in a river. Georgiana fought back and escaped to a neighbouring house. Somehow John Hooper found her and convinced her to continue on their journey to St. Ambroise. John returned to Montreal alone. There he purchased prussic acid, ostensibly to dispose of a troublesome dog. He headed back to St. Ambroise with the intention of placing his wife in an asylum in Montreal. On the way to Montreal, she became ill and died.

After the funeral, John returned to Ottawa. He had, at some point, seen Miss Stapley in Montreal and had proposed marriage to her. John seemed confident that all was well.

It was the telegraph operator at a CPR station near Montreal who changed John's plans. Upon hearing of the death, he recalled that the woman's male companion had called himself Hooper, and that a man of that same name had recently sent a telegram from his office to the agent at Louisville, asking him to look out for a "crazy woman." After talking with the conductor of the train, he took his story to the police to say that he thought the death should be investigated. A Montreal newspaper scooped the sensational story and ran it in the September 22 issue. Other papers picked up the story and it became the scandal of the day. Silas Carpenter, a government detective, was assigned to the case.

Hooper, in the meantime, made a suspicious move when, on September 29, he returned to Port Hope to have his wife's body exhumed, with the intention of having it embalmed. The opening of the grave was in progress when the undertaker, J.T. George, put a stop to it, pointing out that it was illegal without a coroner's order. Hooper then requested Dr. Corbett, the coroner, to hold an inquest. He agreed to this once he had the approval of the County Crown Attorney.

Community interest peaked after it was announced that there would be a coroner's inquest. The jury was composed of 20 well-known Port Hope citizens of the day; crowds gathered at the railway station to catch sight of the witnesses arriving from Montreal and elsewhere; people clamoured to get into the opera house, where the inquest was being held.

During the early stages of the inquest, a number of Port Hope residents were interviewed, and interest and speculation grew after testimony from Dr. Clarke, superintendent of the Rockwood Asylum; the conductor of the train on which the alleged crime was committed; the druggist who sold Hooper the prussic acid; and Miss Stapley, the other woman in the case. Dr. W.J. Douglas of Cobourg had conducted the post-mortem examination and found the death had resulted from unnatural causes. Professor Ellis of Toronto, who had analyzed the contents of the stomach, could find no cause of death there; it was a healthy stomach. However, he admitted that from the symptoms death could have been caused by prussic acid.

The inquest concluded on the night of October 20th, and the jury returned at 2 a.m. on the 21st. At 4 a.m. they delivered this verdict: "We find that the said Georgiana Hooper came to her death at Terrebonne station under suspicious circumstances and from causes unknown to the jury."

Hooper was arrested on a warrant that charged him with the murder of his wife through the administration of prussic acid. He was escorted to Joliette, Quebec, and placed on trial on January 3, 1894. The trail lasted until January 19 and resulted in his acquittal, largely because of the contradictory nature of the medical evidence, on which he was given the benefit of the doubt. However, he was not permitted to go free. He was re-arrested and this time charged with the attempted murder of his wife by drowning. He was tried on this charge at Three Rivers, Quebec, in June 1894, found guilty and sentenced to 25 years. After 10 years of imprisonment he was released on parole and went to live in Winnipeg. Presumably, he never did get together with the comely Alice Stapley.

Since the 1970s Port Hope has become a major tourist centre with historic buildings such as the John David Smith house, 1834 Bluestone House, and St. Mark's Church, which dates back to 1822. It is a well-known fact that the main street of Port Hope is one of the best-preserved examples of late 19th century Ontario. Many beautiful specialty stores attract shoppers from all parts of the province. This is a long way from the simplicity of a trading post, and yet it is, perhaps, a natural progression from the early vision of Peter Smith. The whispering pines haven't disappeared, and the call to settle there can still be heard today.

Port Perry

The settlers of Port Perry must have wondered what they could have possibly done to deserve such devastation when two fires in less than a year (1883–1884) almost destroyed their downtown area.

Powerless to rebuild, as there was not a pound of nails to be had, and hammers and saws were in scarce supply, a public meeting was held. There, the townspeople discussed the situation. The end result was the passing of a bylaw that forbade the construction of wooden buildings within the business section. The building regulations also required that the stores be given a uniform line of frontage. The previous buildings had been erected to suit the fancy of the owner, and the resulting street had been very irregular. The new plan did away with this, and now the stores lined up neatly; few towns the size of Port Perry made such a creditable showing in their business section.

Rebuilding was a busy time. Masons and bricklayers came in from all directions, and in less than a year, the business area was re-established. A steam fire-engine was purchased, and the residents breathed a sigh of relief; Port Perry prospered.

The town of Port Perry had originally been the site of a Native village. In 1821, the first recorded settler, Reuben Crandell, arrived. Others followed. Abner Hurd settled here in 1824. In 1833 Elias Williams purchased Lot 19 in Concession 6, and here he built the first home at the actual site of the future village.

Peter Perry arrived in the district shortly thereafter and eventually surveyed and divided the land into lots. His involvement in the

Courtesy of Scugog Shores Museum

The settlers of Port Perry were no strangers to the destructive power of fire.

Courtesy of Scugog Shores Museum

New building regulations after the fires forbade the construction of wooden buildings within the business district. The regulations also required that the stores be given a uniform line of frontage.

organization of the settlement was reason enough to name the place after him. In 1854 a plank road was built to connect Port Whitby and Lake Scugog. It was originally intended to pass through Prince Albert, but Abner Hurd refused to grant a right-of-way through his property and the road was built closer to Port Perry. As a result Port Perry continued to develop and Prince Albert declined.

Joseph Bigelow and Thomas Paxton spearheaded a project in 1867 to build a railway from Port Whitby to Port Perry. The railway was completed in 1871, and a train station was constructed by Lake Scugog.

Those were the days when 25 steamboats sailed the waters of Lake Scugog. They transported timber, the likes of which could not be found in these parts today. Some trees were used for telegraph poles, while some for tan bark went to Fran A. Cutting at Boston, and some for paving timber was sent to Godson's in Toronto. These paving timbers were made of cedar cut into 15.25 centimetre and 20.25 centimetre (six and eight inch) blocks, and set endwise on the surface of the streets of Toronto.

The price of whiskey at that time was 25 cents a gallon, retail, and 10 cents wholesale. If you felt dry while in town, all you had to do was go to the back of the store, where there would be a pail of whiskey and a tin cup. It was estimated that there were 25 hotels between Manilla and Oshawa in those days.

Port Perry certainly was prosperous, and much of that was due to one man, a visionary with a practical bent, Joseph Bigelow. Joseph and his twin brother Joel left Lindsay in 1851to go to Port Perry. There, they opened a general store under the name "J & J Bigelow." The next year Joseph became the first postmaster of Port Perry. Then he bought a woollen factory and a planing mill. At the mill he also manufactured barrel staves. The factory remained in operation until 1870, when the railway expropriated his land. When the Royal Canadian Bank opened a branch in Port Perry in 1862, Joseph Bigelow became the manager and held the position for six years.

After the building of a three-storey commercial emporium called The Royal Arcade, Bigelow's next project was to promote the construction of the railway. In 1872 he became reeve, and continued to serve in office until 1874. In 1877 he became a justice of the peace and the new owner of an elaborate Italianate house designed and built by H.R. Barber of Oshawa. Joseph planned to build a number of fireplaces with marbleized slate mantelpieces throughout this home, but his wife put her foot down. She felt that fireplaces dirtied, rather than heated, a home! When Joseph died in 1917, at the age of 89, flags flew at half-mast in tribute to a man whose insight and spirit gave reality to his dreams.

Scugog Island, across the lake from Port Perry, extends 16 kilometres (10 miles) in length and measures four kilometres (2.5 miles) wide. The name *Scugog* is a Native word pronounced Scu-a-gog, meaning "submerged or flooded land." Peter Jones, a Native missionary who worked among the Mississauga tribe on the island, called it Whu-yoy-wus-ki-wuh-gog, meaning "shallow muddy lake."

The island was first surveyed in 1816, by Major S. Wilmot. At the time a number of Mississauga Natives inhabited the island and vicinity. A paper, read before the Canadian Institute on January 12, 1889, by A.F. Chamberlain, on the archaeology of Scugog Island, indicated earlier habitation of the island by the Mohawks. There is a legend told that, at one time, the Mississaugas enticed their Mohawk enemies to Paxton's Point, where the Mohawks were subsequently killed in battle.

The first white settler on the island is said to have been Joseph Graxton, who came in 1834. On November 3, 1843, the Mississaugas of Lake Scugog purchased 800 acres of the island that subsequently became known as the Scugog Indian Reserve. The government hired William Taylor to build the Natives 12 houses and three barns. It was an attempt to assimilate them into the ways of non-natives. Some farm machinery was also supplied, but these efforts did not, as they say, "grow corn."

In 1847, according to the missionary's report, the Native population totalled 64. In 1866 the band numbered 38, and other island residents on the island numbered 800 in total.

It was no easy task to settle this island, as cattle had to be transported by barge from the mainland. The first task was to construct a ferry or scow that required two men to each oar. Many tragic stories have been told of the old ferry. Sometime in the 1840s, John Thompson, with George Gilbert and his 17-year-old son, started out on the ferry from Paxton's point to the island. The lake was rougher than expected and the frightened animals started to struggle. A team of horses and a yoke of oxen were being held by young Gilbert, but to no avail. They carried him overboard, and when George Gilbert attempted to save his son, they were both drowned.

Another terrible accident involved John Thompson and his wife. John went to work at the mill, and his wife left the children in the house while she went a short distance to ask a neighbour to stay with her overnight. Although gone only a short time, her house and children went up in smoke.

Scugog was also the setting for a murder with a strange and tragic aftermath. This occurred shortly after the Farewell family had opened a trading post on Washburn's Island on Lake Scugog for barter with the Natives. One day the Farewells left their agent, John Sharp, in charge of the post. When they returned they found him dead. A hunt for the murderer followed, and it was discovered that a Native named Ogetonicut had done the deed. The motive was to avenge the murder of his own brother, Whistling Duck, who had been murdered by a white man. Ogetonicut was arrested, and after a preliminary hearing it was decided that the trial would have to be held at the Newcastle courthouse. Newcastle was the new district town planned for the districts of Northumberland and Durham, to be located at Presqui'le, and the murder had been committed within that judicial district. Ogetonicut was taken to York (Toronto) to await transportation to Presqui'le. A government schooner named the *Speedy* was chartered to take the officials who needed to be present at the trial down the lake. The party was made up of the following persons: Judge Cochrane, Solicitor General Robert Isaac Grey, Sheriff Angus McDonnell, High Bailiff John Fisk, interpreters Cowan and Ruggles, Mr. Herkimer, Captain Paxton, and Ogetonicut.

According to local lore, Ogetonicut's mother travelled from Lake Scugog to the shores of Lake Ontario, near Oshawa, to watch for the *Speedy*. When she caught sight of the vessel sailing by, knowing that her son was onboard, she began to chant against those who had taken him away.

The *Speedy* never reached Newcastle. When, during a snowstorm, it rounded the point near Presqui'le, the ship disappeared without a trace. Neither the *Speedy* nor her passengers were ever seen again!

Many Ontario towns had turbulent beginnings but, like most of them, Port Perry survived its fires, its native struggles, and its developmental challenges. Today, it is a beautiful "bedroom" community. It is much enjoyed as a graceful town with excellent dining, shopping, theatre, and simple beauty — all just an hour from downtown Toronto.

Presqu'ile Provincial Park

Presqu'ile Provincial Park is the fifth-oldest park in Ontario. This park, located just south of Brighton, Ontario, on Highway 2, is 2,300 acres in size — 1,050 acres are covered in water and 1,250 acres are land. This French name means "almost an island." It is a boot-shaped peninsula that juts out 10 kilometres (six miles) into Lake Ontario and was formed when the last of the great glaciers retreated from the Lake Ontario basin about 10,000 years ago. The furthest extension of the peninsula is a limestone island. Gull and High Bluff are two offshore islands to the southwest of the peninsula. An extensive cattail and open water marsh is located to the lee of the peninsula. High Bluff was once connected to Presqu'ile by a sand and gravel bar, but over the years it and Gull Island were both eroded and separated by the pounding waters of Lake Ontario. These two islands were designated as a Wilderness Area under the 1961 Wilderness Areas Act and are off-limits to visitors, because large colonies of gulls and terns nest here.

Presqu'ile itself has forests, marshes, and sand dunes that together support a wide diversity of animal and plant life. Birdwatching is the major attraction. A total of 318 species have been recorded within the park; 130 species are confirmed as breeders. They are among the highest bird totals in Ontario. Migrating waterfowl rest here in the spring on their way north, and sometimes a waterfowl viewing weekend is sponsored by the Ministry of Natural Resources.

Back in 1787, the Mississaugas ceded this area of land to the government. Mississaugas, and other Native tribes before them, gathered here for an annual hunt and honoured this bird habitat as a very sacred place.

Once the government had taken sole ownership of the land, it announced that Presqu'ile would become the site of a proposed town called Newcastle. It was to be the main town for the new district of Northumberland and Durham counties. By 1804, the first public building, a court house, had been built and its first trial was scheduled — a murder trial.

The accused was an Ojibwa native charged with the murder of a fur trader near the settlement of Port Perry. Unbeknownst to all concerned, this trial was an omen of things to come.

On October 7, 1804, the schooner *Speedy* departed from York (Toronto) with the prisoner and several influential people who were to be at the trial. As fate would have it, the crew, passengers, and prisoner vanished. According to the stories, the *Speedy* had reached Presqu'ile on October 9 and was rounding the point when it floundered in a sudden snowstorm and sank without a trace — no survivors, no bodies, no ship, no flotsam, and no jetsam. In fact, no trace of the *Speedy* has ever been found despite numerous attempts by divers in the Presqu'ile waters. What could possibly have happened? Was it magic; was it a curse? (See the story about Port Perry for more on this strange incident.)

Like the *Speedy*, the district town of Newcastle also vanished. In 1805 the Government of Upper Canada abandoned their plans for Presqu'ile with an accompanying declaration that the designated townsite of Newcastle was not convenient.

In 1840 a lighthouse was built at the tip of the peninsula to guide boats to safety, since Presqu'ile offered one of the best harbours on Lake Ontario. Today, the lighthouse keeper's quarters house a museum. After the disappearance of the *Speedy* and the cancellation of the town of Newcastle, Presqu'ile regained some prestige as a recreational centre. In 1905 construction of the Presqu'ile Hotel and some summer cottages ushered in the age of tourism.

The act of fate was a blessing in disguise when it stepped in to preserve this unusual, beautiful, and natural setting for recreation, this sanctuary where birds and people meet.

Sault Ste. Marie

Prior to the arrival of the Europeans, the Ojibwa of the 17th century called the present site of Sault Ste. Marie *Pawating*, which means "turbulent waters." The Jesuit missionaries arrived here in 1634 and named the location Sault Ste. Marie. It must indeed have felt like true virgin land in all of that natural beauty.

In 1671 Daumont de St. Lusson took possession of the entire interior of the continent for the French. An historic ceremony, to mark the event, was held at Sault Ste. Marie. For the next several years, Sault Ste. Marie was the major centre of French activity in Upper Canada.

The first fort in the area was constructed by the French at St. Ignace, in 1696. Five years later, the garrison was moved to what is now Detroit. The French re-established the fort at the tip of the lower peninsula. Occupation of the fort, by the French, continued until the fall of Quebec. By 1767 the fort was occupied by the British until the garrison was ordered to move to Michilimackinac Island. The British government kept possession of the fort until after the close of the War of Independence. Fort St. Joseph, built in 1796, was located 48 kilometres (30 miles) east of Sault Ste. Marie.

The North-West Company established a trading post at Sault Ste. Marie in 1783. In 1814 the village was attacked by the American forces during the War of 1812. The Americans torched the North-West Company post, and most of the village was burned to the ground. The company rebuilt after the war, and by 1821 became the Hudson's Bay Company.

The first recorded British settler to become a citizen of Sault Ste. Marie was Joseph Wilson. The government sent Wilson there in 1843 to carry out the duties of Indian agent, customs officer, postmaster, general military officer, and government contractor. Two years later, surveys of Sault Ste. Marie and the townships in the vicinity were made, and these lands were opened for general settlement by pioneers. However, land to be surrendered by the Ojibwa was needed in order to facilitate the government's objective: mining interests in the area and settlement.

The development of the mining industry created a strong government incentive for negotiations of land surrender from the Ojibwa. Many settlement sites were located close to mineral deposits, particularly copper. Prospecting, surveying, and technical teams scouted the countryside for mineral deposits. Interest increased with the development of successful mining operations on the upper Michigan Peninsula. Many entrepreneurs believed that copper deposits in particular would be found on both sides of the Upper Great Lakes.

By 1845 the Crown Lands Department had created prospecting regulations and licensing to determine the boundaries of mining claims and the price of lands that contained base metals. In May 1846 the department issued 34 licences to prospect for minerals on the north shore of Lake Superior.

One of the first companies to seek the opportunities of the north was the Montreal Mining Company. This English company purchased numerous mining locations totalling 466 square kilometres (180 miles); one single location extended eight kilometres (five miles) long and more than three kilometres (two miles) wide. In 1848 their holdings at Bruce Mines on Lake Huron reported that 1,475 tonnes of copper ore had been extracted. The government made a decision to send out its own surveyors to locate other sources of minerals.

The Natives were watching the antics of these newcomers and warned them to leave untouched any land that had been set aside for Native use. One surveyor in particular was threatened by Chief Shinguakouse of Garden River. The Chief wrote to the governor-general on June 10, 1846. In his letter Shinguakouse referred to his service to the British in the War of 1812, and he reminded the governor-general that he had been promised at that time that he would be able to live "unmolested forever." He felt the promise had been broken with the arrival of men into his region of land.

In 1849 two gentlemen, Anderson and Vidal, were sent by the government to the northern shores of Lake Huron and Lake Superior to determine the strength of any Native claim to the land. Their report stated that "the claim of the present occupants of this tract derived from their forefathers, who have from time immemorial hunted upon it." They further noted "that the claim was unquestionably as good as that of any of the tribes who had received compensation for the cession of their rights in other parts of the Province; and therefore they were entitled to similar remuneration."

The government was slow to act, and some people decided to take matters into their own hands. In November of that same year, a group of First Nations people and Metis, led by the white entrepreneur Allan Macdonell, travelled from Sault Ste. Marie along the shore of Lake Superior for about 320 kilometres (200 miles) to Mica Bay. Upon reaching Mica Bay, they attacked the mining installations of the Quebec Mining Company. Reports of the armed force, led by Macdonell, varied widely, as few as 30 and as many as 100 people. The company agent, John Bonner, surrendered the mining site without any resistance.

The government sent 100 soldiers to suppress the revolt. In December Macdonell and another participant, Metcalfe, were arrested, as were two Metis and two Ojibwa chiefs including Shinguakouse. They were sent to York (Toronto) to stand trial. Eventually, they all were all released.

The Anderson-Vidal report and the incident at Mica Bay prompted the government to settle the northwestern land question quickly. William Benjamin Robinson was appointed to achieve this goal. The government wanted him to buy as much land as possible, but not to settle for less than "the north shore of Lake Huron and the mining sites along the eastern shore of Lake Superior." It was Robinson's intention during these meetings to acquire all the lands on both Lake Huron and Lake Superior for 4,000 British pounds ($10,000) in cash, and a perpetual annuity of 1,000 British pounds for the region.

W.B. Robinson was able to complete two agreements in September 1850 for virtually the whole of the Upper Canadian northwest for government use. These agreements are generally referred to as the Robinson-Huron Treaty and the Robinson-Superior Treaty. The first agreement called for the cession of the Lake Huron shoreline, including the islands, from

Matchedash Bay to Batchewana Bay, and inland as far as the height of the land. The latter agreement gave the crown the shoreline of Lake Superior, including islands, from Batchewana Bay to the Pigeon River, inland as "far as the height of land," which probably meant to the horizon. The first contained 92,500 square kilometres (35,700 miles) of land, inhabited by a total Native population of 1,240; the latter was occupied by 1,422 Natives and covered 43,250 square kilometres (16,700 miles) of territory.

Two years prior to the Native land settlement, the first dock on the Canadian side of Sault Ste. Marie was begun by a Mr. Garfield, at the foot of Spring Street. Then it was not long before the first lake steamer, the *Gore*, engaged in a regular passenger and freight service from southern points on Georgian Bay to points along the North Shore. The *Dime*, so named for the price of the fare from Michigan to Canada, was the first steam ferry to run between the two Saults.

The first settlers in the area were connected primarily to the fur trade and came from Ireland, France, Scotland, and England. When the fur trade declined, the settlement became little more than a steamboat landing. In 1857 the population of non-native settlers was 300.

Sault Ste. Marie was incorporated as a village in 1871, and in 1887 as a town. That same year, the Canadian Pacific Railway and the International Bridge over the rapids were constructed; this provided Sault Ste. Marie with active transport connections to a greater area. In 1895 the Ship Canal was opened for traffic. Prosperity led to city status by 1912.

At the turn of the century, a rather enterprising soul by the name of Francis H. Clergue arrived in the area. He was a shrewd man and quickly realized the marvelous potential of the area; within a few years, he had developed numerous industries. The Power Canal was enlarged, the Pulp Mill and the Hudson Bay Railway were constructed, and the iron ore mines of the Michipicoten District were developed. The steel industry was established at Sault Ste. Marie, following the incorporation of The Algoma Steel Company Limited in May 1901, and the first standard steel rails to be made in Canada were rolled in May 1902.

Rapid industrial development attracted European immigrants. Italians, Finnish, French, and Polish arrived, eager to work. Since the end of the Second World War, many Dutch and German families have called Sault Ste. Marie their home.

The 20-million-dollar International Bridge connecting the two "Soos," as they are affectionately termed, was officially opened in 1963 by Governor George Romney of Michigan and Premier John Roberts of Ontario.

Ernest Hemingway once remarked in the *Toronto Star Weekly* that the best rainbow trout fishing in the world was in the rapids at the Canadian Soo. To this day, St. Mary's Rapids is rated once of the best trout rivers in the world, right on the waterfront of Sault Ste. Marie.

Tourism is a major industry for the city of Sault Ste. Marie today. A very popular attraction in the area is the famous one-day wilderness train tour of Agawa Canyon. Tourists climb aboard to relax and recline in their seats as they roll past beautiful pristine waters and the incredible gorges of Algoma Central Country. It is a 180-kilometre (114-mile) trip from Sault Ste. Marie to the Agawa Canyon, where a two-hour stopover provides an opportunity to photograph waterfalls and rocky cliffs, walk well-groomed nature trails, or climb up to the lookout for an awesome view of the canyon floor below.

This incredible opportunity to see the magnificent geographic features of the Laurentian Shield is available in every season, which is an unusual opportunity in the north.

One can still experience what the Jesuits felt: a virgin land, a land still unconquered, strong, beautiful, defiant, awesome. We are blessed indeed to have this in our midst.

Scarborough

On August 4, 1793, Lady Simcoe, the wife of Lieutenant-Governor Simcoe, while riding in a boat on Lake Ontario, recorded this in her diary: "We came within sight of what is named in the map, The Highlands. The shore is extremely bold and has the appearance of Chalk Cliffs, appearing so well that we talked of building a summer residence there and calling it Scarborough." Surveyor Augustus Jones was also particularly struck by the majesty of the cliffs and had earlier been responsible for naming the area "The Highlands."

On August 27 of that year, on the occasion of the naming of York, the great grey cliffs to the east, so similar to those of the English Yorkshire town, became known as Scarborough.

The Scarborough Bluffs run along Lake Ontario for approximately 9.5 kilometres (six miles). These cliffs contain a vivid record, in the uppermost 60 metres (200 feet), of the last stages of the Great Ice Age. Under layers of glacial till are 45 metres (150 feet) of sediments called the Scarborough beds. They are made up of 18 metres (60 feet) of stratified sand and 27 metres (90 feet) of peaty clay. The clay area contains some wood, leaves, mosses, and the remains of 72 species of beetles, all but two of which are now extinct.

Jonathan Gates was one of the early pioneers here. In 1815 he cleared the land and settled east of the gully that descends to the lake south of the junction of Kingston and Bellamy Roads. Gates wasn't the first person to settle in the area. Only as recently as 1956, when the Miller Paving Company turned up some skeletons, has the earlier settlement history come to light. From 1956–1958 the Royal Ontario Museum ethnologist, Walter Kenyon, excavated the site and charted a village of about one acre in size. Radio-carbon testing showed that the village had been occupied around 1,125 A.D. Evidence found during the dig suggested that it belonged to a pre-Iroquoian group called Glen Meyer. Within the palisade area, archaeologists traced the outline of five multiple-family longhouses. They ranged from 11.5 metres to 18 metres (38 to 60 feet) in length and from six metres to eight metres (20 to 27 feet) in width. A steam-shovel operator cutting into Taboris Hill, at the east side of Bellamy Road north of Lawrence Avenue, exposed an ancient Native burial pit. Two sites, together containing the bones of 472 people, were found. In a solemn ceremony on October 20, 1956, these bones were reburied by the chiefs of the Six Nations.

In the years following 1793, many shrewd government officials and army officers of York obtained generous grants of land in the Township of Scarborough. These landowners were speculators and wanted the sites for future development, or resale at a profit.

In 1796 the highlands of Scarborough caught the eye of a Scottish stone mason by the name of David Thomson. He had come from Dumfriesshire by the way of Niagara and was employed in the construction of the new government buildings of York. Thompson searched beyond the Don River for a home for his family. When he travelled 20 kilometres (12 miles) on a Native trail that wound northeast from the 40 houses on the shore of the bay called York, and 4.5 kilometres (three miles) back from the bluffs, he found his land of promise on the banks of Highland Creek. There he built a lone log cottage not far from the present-day Scarborough Hospital.

Down by the bluffs, at the foot of what is now Markham Road, William Cornell moved his family from the schooner, on which they had lived for a summer, to the heights, where he built a home. In the course of two years, he cleared and planted Scarborough's first orchard. During the winter he travelled to Kingston to purchase millstones in exchange for a fine span of colts and returned by sled to Highland Creek. There he built the first grist and saw mill.

Another courageous Scarborough pioneer was Sarah Ashbridge, a widow who arrived at York from Philadelphia, in 1793. Together with her two sons and three daughters, she settled near the mouth of the Don River. She later began clearing the 300 acres of granted land that extended north from the bluffs, east of Midland Avenue.

In 1803 Stephen Perril built the first brick house in Scarborough. Around 1834 a carpenter named Thomas Adams, who had arrived from Vermont in 1808, built a sailing vessel named the *Mary Ann*, at the mouth of Highland Creek. The vessel provided a tremendous service to the farmers for many years by transporting potash, grain, and shingles to York. On her return trip, the vessel brought flour, salt, and lime to the settlers of Scarborough. By 1830 the population of Scarborough had reached 135.

During the mid-1800s, three gristmills and 23 sawmills operated along the banks of Highland Creek and the Rouge River. Several villages flourished at the crossroads: Highland Creek, Malvern, Ellesmere, Wexford, and Woburn.

Scarborough was formally incorporated as a municipality in 1850. This was the beginning of local self-government. In 1910 Sir Eugene O'Keefe of the Toronto brewing family donated $500,000 for the construction of St. Augustine's Seminary. A lovely site of more than 100 acres was acquired on the south side of Kingston Road, east of Midland Avenue. The imposing structure of St. Augustine's Seminary, crowned by a lofty dome, still stands on the bluffs high above Lake Ontario. Opened and dedicated on August 28, 1913, the seminary has trained at least 1,400 students for the priesthood, over a 50-year span.

Following the end of the First World War, the suburbanization of southern Scarborough grew steadily. By 1925 the population of Scarborough was 15,783 and by 1930 it had grown to 18,351.

At the end of the Second World War, the influx of immigrants from Europe opened a new chapter in the history of Scarborough. Over the next 20 years, farm after farm was devoured by bulldozers. Row upon row of closely packed houses and towering apartment buildings sprang up like a new crop in a farmer's field. Factories emerged and Scarborough quickly became Ontario's fifth-largest municipality, with a population of 224,000.

One of the most extraordinary cultural sites in Scarborough is the Guild Inn. The Guild of All Arts, its original name, began in 1932 when

Rosa and Spencer Clark purchased the central property of 40 acres, once known as Ranelagh Park, located on Eglington (the original spelling). They resided in the main building, originally constructed by Gerald Harold C. Bickford, to be his country home.

During the depression the Clarks hoped to help those difficult years by stimulating interest in the arts and crafts, and by indicating ways in which a livelihood might be gained. Within a year there were shops and studios with sculptures, batiks, weavings, tooled leather, ceramics, pewter and copper, wrought-iron, and woodwork. In succeeding years more of the fine and lively arts were added.

Attracted by the activities and the beauty of the setting, atop the Scarborough Bluffs, visitors arrived in increasing numbers. Dining facilities were added and guest rooms followed until the Guild facilities became a flourishing country inn, uniquely situated in the midst of its arts and crafts activities.

During the winter of 1942–43, the Guild became an official naval base, HMCS Bytown II, where the first group of Wrens were trained. Shortly thereafter, the entire property was requisitioned as a specialized military hospital. Used entirely for nervous disorders, it was known as "Scarborough Hall."

When the Guild was returned to the Clarks in 1947, some of the craftsmen had established themselves elsewhere, some had been lost in the war, but others did return. The Guild's guests and visitors came back in even greater numbers. It was necessary to expand the accommodation, and the Guild Inn name became even more widely known.

The grounds of the Guild are adorned with a collection of historic architecture. More than 40 years of effort by Spencer Clark has resulted in saving important fragments of about 60 buildings; items like Sir Frederick Banting's fireplace and the original steps of Osgoode Hall can be found here. A grindstone, made in Ireland circa 1860, was brought to Canada by the Goldie family of Galt, and it is now on the grounds of the inn.

In 1978 the Metropolitan Toronto and Region Conservation Authority, acting for Metropolitan Toronto and the Provincial Government, purchased the Guild and its surrounding land.

Today the Guild Inn is closed. The future of the inn is overshadowed by thoughts of demolition and future development.

Scarborough, throughout its history, has been identified with the stark beauty of its bluffs. The silence, stillness, and the boldness here that caught the attention of Lady Simcoe and the fancy of David Thomson can still be seen and felt. If you walk beneath the cliffs along the lake, you can ignore the modern development around you and gaze over the lake and up the rough-hewn bluff even as our forefathers did. There is a day park there which, fortunately, makes this beautiful sight still available to everyone.

The Ghost of Tom Thomson — Canoe Lake, Algonquin Park

When a woman or man is murdered, their soul often remains the prisoner of circumstance. They remain in the vicinity of the crime. For nearly a century, the death of Tom Thomson on Canoe Lake, in 1917, has remained a mystery. Was it accidental drowning or was it murder? The existence of his spirit on Canoe Lake could support the theory of murder. You be the judge.

Tom Thomson was born in Claremont, Ontario, on August 4, 1877. At the age of two months, his parents, along with his six brothers and sisters, moved to the town of Leigh near Owen Sound on Georgian Bay.

As a young boy, he thoroughly enjoyed the outdoors, fishing in the bay, swimming, and boating. Tom had an ear for music and played the violin, mandolin, and coronet. He was also fascinated by birds, the colour of leaves in the autumn, and flowers in the spring. According to his brother, George, he paid keen attention to the seasonal movements of animals. As a teenager he was strongly built and stood almost two metres (six feet). Judge Little, author of *The Tom Thomson Mystery*, said, "Conversely he couldn't find satisfaction in study; he neither finished high school nor completed a machinists' apprenticeship started in his late teens at Owen Sound. He also attempted, but never completed, a business course at Chatham."

It was in 1901, at the age of 24, that Tom took his first step toward a career in art. He followed his brothers, George and Henry, to Seattle, and there joined a commercial art studio where George had begun a year earlier. There Tom explored the territory of his imagination; there he began experimenting with crayon and then watercolour sketches. Some mention has been given to an unsuccessful romance with a woman while he was in Seattle, which fostered his return to Toronto, in 1905. There he found employment with a commercial art firm.

In 1911, he acquired a new job with the firm of Grip Limited. It was here that he made contact with other kindred spirits — J.E.H. MacDonald, Arthur Lismer, Fred Varley, Tom MacLean, A.Y. Jackson, and Frank Carmichael. At 34 Tom had begun to do sketches and oil paintings around Toronto, near the Don Valley, Rosedale Ravine, Scarlet Road, Old Mill, and Lambton.

In early 1912 Tom made his first trek to picturesque Canoe Lake in Algonquin Park. Between 1913 and 1917, he painted in Algonquin from spring break, up until late fall. The majority of his works were inspired here, including *Northern River*, *West Wind*, *Spring Ice*, *Jack Pine*, and *Northern Lights*. He painted 24 major canvasses and made more than 300 sketches.

Judge William T. Little quoted park ranger Mark Robinson — who first met Thomson in the spring of 1912 — in his book, *The Tom Thomson Mystery*: "One evening as I went to Canoe Lake, a couple of other rangers had joined me. It was quite routine in those days for park rangers to inspect all newcomers coming into the park because poaching was a major offence and a common occurrence in the park. As the train came in and drew to a stop, a tall, fine-looking man with a packsack on his back stepped off the train. The stranger inquired where he could find a place to stay, and where he could get a good bed and good eats. I explained to him that the Algonquin Hotel was a short distance away and Mowat Lodge was nearby. A man by the name of Fraser served good meals there and had excellent beds. Tom said 'that was the place for him.'"

Mowat Lodge became his home away from home. In the ensuing years, Tom lived with the Frasers as one of the family. He even designed a cover for the Frasers' booklet to announce Mowat Lodge. Tom was, nevertheless, a loner, and often canoed out into the lake and disappeared for days on end, painting and fishing to his heart's content. He was an amiable man with rugged, lean, muscular good looks. Tom was well-liked by most who met him and enjoyed the company of others at the many parties in the area.

Courtesy of Jane Loftus

Fishing was a passion of Tom Thomson. No one could explain why a length of fishing line was wrapped 16–17 times around his left ankle at the time of his death.

Mark Robinson pointed out that Tom earned his way in the park by purchasing a guide license and subsequently led parties of fishermen through the park. He often tented on the east side of Canoe Lake, opposite Mowat Landing, just north of Hayhurst's Point.

In April 1917 Tom arrived at Canoe Lake for the last time. On July 7 of that year, Tom and a number of local cottage residents met at George Rowe's cabin for some merriment. Drinking at these social events usually led to storytelling. The topic of the war arose, and Tom spoke of his determination to join up as a fire ranger. His earlier attempts to join had been thwarted because of his flat feet. That night Martin Bletcher, who was considered to have a bad temperament, always exacerbated by heavy drinking, arrived at the party.

Judge Little wrote, "One young American cottager in particular, Martin Bletcher, who was of German background, was most outspoken regarding the progress of the war and his forecast of ultimate German supremacy. During the early summer Tom and Martin seemed to share a mutual dislike. These two men, during this Saturday evening, were actually prevented from coming to blows only by the good-natured efforts of the guides. On leaving the cabin before midnight, Bletcher hurled a final threat, 'Don't get in my way if you know what's good for you.'"

A love triangle can be a source of great pain and jealousy. Secret love is even more entangling and complex. Winnie Trainor was, by all accounts, a beautiful, mysterious woman. Hidden to most, Winnie and Tom shared a secret love. Judge Little said, "Not until Miss Trainor's death in 1962 has it been known, authoritatively, that Thomson intended to marry her. Did Martin Bletcher resent Tom's visits to Winnie Trainor, just next door to him, during those long summer evenings? Did Tom resent Martin's presence so close to Miss Trainor's cottage?"

Terence Trainor McCormick, the nephew and beneficiary of Miss Trainor's estate, once stated, about the letters written between Winnie and Tom, "… the correspondence gave undisputable evidence that Tom and my Aunt were engaged to be married." Their covenant remained a secret known only to them.

On July 8, 1917, it was a rather dull and wet morning. Shannon Fraser and Tom threw a line in the water at the dam between Joe and Canoe Lakes. Mark Robinson caught sight of the men. Tom waved to Mark and called, "Howdy, Mark." Mark acknowledged the greeting. It would be the last time he saw Tom alive.

Tom returned to his quarters, where he gathered up his tackle box and a loaf of bread and some bacon from Mowat Lodge. He bid farewell to Shannon as his canoe cut a path across the waters of Canoe Lake. Shannon watched Tom disappear past Little Wapomeo Island, only 1.5 kilometres (one mile) away.

The following day Martin Bletcher casually remarked to some guests at Mowat Lodge that he had spotted an upturned canoe between Little and Big Wapomeo Islands. Apparently, he and his sister had not stopped, but continued on for an afternoon fishing excursion. On their return trip, the canoe had disappeared.

No one seemed too concerned about such a report. It was a strange reaction by such a small community of residents, who all knew the boats on the lake. Judge Little added, "Furthermore, Canoe Lake residents considered it strange that Martin Bletcher could not have recognized Thomson's grey-green canoe with a metal strip on the keel side; it was known to everyone on Canoe Lake at the time."

Charlie Scrim found the craft the following morning, behind Big Wapomeo Island. Mark Robinson said, "Contrary to some people who may tell you the canoe was floating right side up, there was none of his equipment in the canoe, except his portaging paddle, which was lashed in position for carrying, and the ground sheet with bread and bacon in the bow section. There were no fishing poles, no gear; even his small axe was gone."

Robinson immediately reported to Park Superintendent Bartlett who authorized a search. Tom's brother, George, was contacted. He arrived at Canoe Lake on July 12. Dynamite was exploded in the lake without the desired results — no body surfaced.

The sharp eyes and minds of guides George Rowe and Charlie Scrim noted that Tom's own working paddle was missing. Especially strange was how the portaging paddle was lashed in a position to portage. It had been knotted in a most unorthodox way. Only an inexperienced canoeist would fashion such a knot. Thomson was an expert canoeist and outdoorsman.

On July 14 George Thomson gathered up a number of Tom's sketches and caught the train back to New York. He felt there was little he could do.

On the morning of July 15, 1917, Dr. G.W. Howland spotted something lying low in the water by Hayhurst Point on the east shore of Canoe Lake. At first he thought it was a loon. At the same time, George Rowe and Lowrie Dickson were paddling down the middle of the lake when they saw the doctor hailing them. The canoeists aimed for the object. It was Tom. He was dead.

They towed the body to a campsite on Big Wapomeo, approximately 300 metres (100 yards) ahead. There at Big Wap, a campout halfway down the west side of the lake, they tied the body to tree roots in a shallow. The guides then notified Dr. Howland and Mark Robinson, who contacted Superintendent Bartlett.

Dr. A.E. Ranney, a coroner living in North Bay, was notified. He did not arrive on the train the next day. Robinson was frantic and informed his superintendent that something needed to be done with the body. It was not right to leave it in the blazing sun. The superintendent told Mark to have Dr. Howland examine the body. Dr. Howland was a Toronto medical doctor and a professor of neurology at the University of Toronto who was vacationing on Wapomeo Island. Mark then ordered a casket and rough box for the burial.

On the morning of July 17, Dr. Howland examined the deceased. Mark helped to remove a length of fishing line that was wrapped 16 or 17 times around Tom's left ankle. That was odd. There was no water in the lungs. Across the left temple was a mark that looked as though he had been struck with the edge of a paddle. The doctor's report read, "A bruise on left temple the size of 4 inches long, no other sign of external marks visible on body, air issuing from mouth, some bleeding from right ear. Cause of death, drowning."

Tom was placed in a casket and moved to the mainland for a hurried funeral. A small congregation of Canoe Lake residents and guides, including Miss Trainor, caught the evening train for Huntsville. She would never again greet her lover by the water's edge. Or would she?

A short time later, a telegram arrived to the attention of Shannon Fraser. It was a request by Mr. H.W. Churchill, a Huntsville undertaker, to exhume the body. Apparently, the family had requested that Tom be interred near the family home at Leith, Ontario. At 8:00 p.m. Fraser met the eastbound train at Canoe Lake Station. Churchill got off the train wearing a dark suit and bowler hat. He informed Fraser that he had a metal casket with him and asked that Fraser give him a hand to put it on his wagon.

With a call to the horses they were off. Fraser was stunned to learn that Churchill was going to remove the body that very night. It all seemed very strange. Fraser remarked that he couldn't get any help until the next day.

Judge Little quoted the following conversation: "The undertaker replied, 'I don't need any help, just get me a good digging shovel, a lantern and a crow bar and I'll do the rest.'

'Here we are,' announced Shannon. 'Do you still want to do this job tonight without any help?'

'Just pick me up about midnight and I'll be ready,' replied the undertaker."

Fraser returned at midnight to give Churchill a hand to place the casket on the rear baggage floor of the coach and transport the body to the train station. Judge Little highlighted an oddity that occurred: "Fraser was to comment a number of times later, 'It just didn't impress me the weight was distributed the way it should be with a body in it.'"

Courtesy of Jane Loftus

Judge Little had to see for himself if Tom Thomson was still buried at Canoe Lake. From left to right: Leonard Gibson, Little, W.J. Eastaugh, and Frank Braught starting to dig. To their amazement they found a body in Thomson's grave.

Judge Little also documented Mark Robinson's comments: "The Superintendent called me up and said, 'Go down to the cemetery and if they haven't filled the grave in, fill it in.' I went down. Now, in one corner of the grave was a hole. I wouldn't say it would be more than 20 inches wide and about a depth of 18 inches. God forgive me if I'm wrong but I still think Thomson's body is over there (Mark pointed to the hillside gravesite where Tom was originally interred)."

In the 1950s Judge Little and three other men, Jack Eastaugh, Leonard Gibson, and Frank Braught decided to investigate the Thomson mystery themselves. They firmly believed Tom was still buried in the Canoe Lake Cemetery. The judge was convinced he had been murdered. Armed with shovels and axes, the men began to clear the underbrush. At six feet (two metres) they found nothing. Then Jack called out from beside a spruce tree. There were depressions 3 feet (one metre) wide in the ground. They began to dig. They struck pay dirt. The shovel found the remains of a rough pine box. No name was inscribed on the box. There was no evidence of metal remnants, such as buttons, belt buckle, shoe nails or clothing.

Judge Little described the scene: "We saw parts of the casket lining and what appeared to be possibly a cotton or light canvas shroud. We recalled that, after Tom's examination by Dr. Howland, the body was immediately placed in a casket wrapped only in a shroud due to the removal of clothes related to the advanced state of decomposition of the body. We also discovered a hole in the skull in the region of the temple which coincided with the region indicated at both the inquest and in Mark Robinson's observations of a blow to the temple."

A short time later, Dr. Henry Ebbs and Dr. Noble Sharpe of the Ontario Provincial Criminal Laboratory arrived at Canoe Lake. They gathered the skeletal remains and photographed the skull with its puncture at the temple.

Dr. Sharpe later concluded, "The bones were definitely male. Calculations from humerus, femur and tibia gave an estimated height of 5'8". These bones suggested also a robust, well-muscled person."

Professor J.C.B Grant, of the Department of Anthropology, University of Toronto, was asked for his opinion. He stated: "The skeleton was of a male, strong, height 5'8" plus or minus 2", age in late 20s and of Mongolian type, either Indian or nearly full-breed Indian."

Further studies were made of the skull, including x-rays. According to Judge Little, "X-ray of the skull before emptying out the sand showed no bullet in the skull and none found in the sand after emptying. The hole in the left temple region is nearly three-quarters of an inch [less than two centimetres] in diameter. The inner plate opening is slightly wider showing a slight bevelling. No radiating fractures were seen in X-ray.

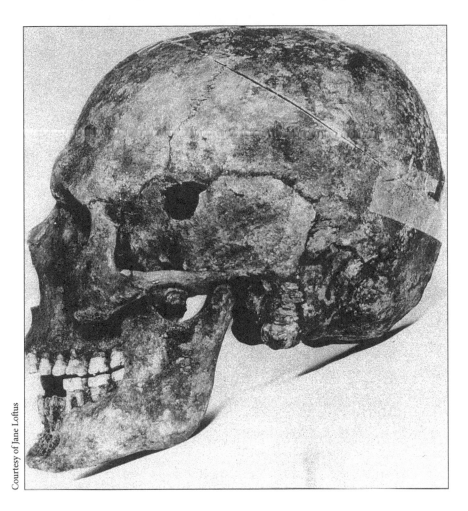

Courtesy of Jane Loftus

The skull removed from Thomson's grave indicates a hole at the temple, coinciding with the injury sustained by the artist.

There was no injury on the inner table of the skull opposite the hole where a bullet would impinge. The orbital plate and nasal bones were so intact that no bullet could have escaped from the skull." Therefore, the hole in the temple was not the result of a bullet wound.

Professor Eric Linnel of the Department of Neuropathology concluded, "The wound, however, though definitely not due to a bullet, could be caused by a sharp instrument such as a pick, a narrow hammer head." (Maybe a paddle?)

Judge Little responded to the investigation: "The foot of the grave in which the bones were found was 21 feet [seven metres] due north of the corner of the fence surrounding the two marked graves. This is, certainly, approximately where Mr. Thomson was buried originally. There is nothing to prove that the opened grave is not the same as Mr. Thomson's, and the coffin is just as his was said to be."

Why so much conflicting information? Did this group of men really dig up the remains of Tom Thomson? There should have been no body at all!

Jane Loftus, the daughter of the late Judge Little, states, "My father always believed the body they found in Canoe Lake Cemetery was that of Tom Thomson."

In 1935 Miss Blodwen Davies, an official of the Saskatchewan Art Board, published a biography of Tom Thomson. It was while doing the research for the book that she investigated his death. She concluded: "I came away from my investigation with the conviction there had been foul play. I tried to get the Ontario Government to open an investigation, but they said it had all happened so long ago, it was best to leave it alone."

Miss Davies spent the rest of her life pursuing the mystery. She once wrote, concerning the testimony at the inquest: "No one remarked that only a living body could be bruised or bleed, or that Thomson's lungs were filled with air, not with water."

A questionnaire she used with Mark Robinson is reprinted courtesy of the Archives of Canada, Ottawa:

> Question: How deep was the water in which Thomson
>   was found?
> Answer: About 30 feet [10 metres].
> Question: How far was it from shore?
> Answer: 125 yards [120 metres].
> Question: Was his fishing rod and line found?
> Answer: No.
> Question: Do you think it was his own line which was
>   wound around his ankle?
> Answer: It might have been his own line but not his
>   regular fishing line.

Question: Did you see a mark on his forehead and if so, what was it like?

Answer: A slight bruise over the eyebrow.

Question: Did the Bletchers aid in the search for Thomson?

Answer: They did on the lake. They did not search in the woods, as far as I know.

Question: Did they make any attempt to direct the search?

Answer: No. They were very quiet in every way.

Little added, "Who was it that struck him a blow across the temple — and was it done with edge of a paddle blade? — that sent the blood spurting from his ear?"

So many of Thomson's friends were puzzled over his death. Many did not believe that he had drowned. Miss Davies added, "Why did Thomson's body take eight days to rise in a shallow lake in the middle of July? Bodies that have been in warm summer waters usually rise after a couple of days, due to bloating. Could the fishing line bound round the lower left leg have been tied to some weighty object such as a stone?

As Little noted, "If Tom struck his head on rocks after death, how could the body bleed? Bodies do not bruise or bleed after death. This man was not accident prone; he was a canoeist of exceptional skill. The weather and water conditions were calm. It is difficult to believe he just fell out of his canoe and received a severe wound to his head."

In a letter Miss Margaret Howland wrote to Judge Little on May 2, 1969, she stated, "My father, the late Dr. Howland, in subsequent discussion mentioned the fact that there was a possibility that the drowning of Tom Thomson was not accidental."

Tom Thomson has never left Canoe Lake. Speculation says that he was murdered and he was in love. Just ask Mrs. Northway and Canadian artist, Lawren Harris, who resided in the park in the summer of 1931. They believe he appeared on the waters that year.

Judge Little recorded their experience: "It had been a happy day and ever so lazy. At dusk we were coming home, tired, rested, and at peace with the world. It was a tremendously still evening, you could hear the silence against your ear. The hills made strange, statuesque figures against the haunting orange of the western sky, while the first star set its light akindle, as an alter lamp of the universe against the canopy of the after glow. Even my guide's tales ceased, and through my mind drifted, fragments of harmonies as if heard from a far way 'cello.' Suddenly the voice of my guide shattered the silence. 'They're coming out to meet us from the portage.'

"And turning toward the sunset I saw a man kneeling in a canoe that slowly came towards us. 'So they are,' I answered. 'I guess we are pretty late.'

"My guide turned from his course in order that we might better meet our herald, now a little less than 100 yards[90 metres] away. I raised my voice and called, and waved my hand, while my guide kept paddling toward the camper. But there was no response, for even as we looked, the canoe and its paddler, without warning or sound, vanished into nothingness, and on the undisturbed lake were only our lonely selves and the shrieking of a loon."

Miss Northway added some observations her mother had left out of the story: "As my mother was coming into the bay by the portage, she saw a canoe and a paddler in a yellow shirt. 'They're coming out from the portage to meet us,' said the guide. The man waved and the guide waved back. Then the paddler, canoe and all, completely vanished.

"My father and Mr. Taylor Statten, being practical people, on hearing the tale, insisted it had been a mirage, but Lawren Harris was sure it was the spirit of Tom Thomson. His rationale was that those who depart before their time continue to haunt the lands they loved.

"My mother was inclined to accept Lawren's interpretation, much to my father's disgust. A point that was much discussed, but never settled, what colour of shirt was Tom wearing when he was drowned?"

For years people have reported seeing a phantom canoeist travelling the waters of Algonquin Park. One moment you see a man paddling a canoe across the way and in the next, he vanishes. Many eyewitness accounts refer to the canoeist as Tom Thomson. One witness to such an event was drawn to paint the experience.

Doug Dunford is a professional artist, best known for his ability to capture the symbols of Muskoka life in high-realist style. He lives in the Muskokas.

Early in his career he was given one of A.Y. Jackson's easels and old chairs. These were his first connections to the Group of Seven painters, but others followed.

In the summer of 1980, Doug found himself painting a new sign for Algonquin Park. For two weeks he immersed himself in the natural beauty of the park.

One evening a social gathering took place at a cottage on Canoe Lake. Doug recalled: "The next morning I decided to go down to the dock. A thick mist was enshrouding Canoe Lake. I just stood on the dock with my camera hanging around my neck, looking. Then I heard this trickling sound like a paddle in the water. Suddenly a person in a canoe emerged from the mist. We made eye contact, and then he turned and vanished. For some unknown reason I took his picture just before he turned and disappeared, as abruptly and mystically as he had appeared.

"In that moment I sensed a strange energy. It took me off guard. I have felt that strange feeling before. I don't know why I took the picture and began to second-guess the experience. Had it really happened? Would there be anything on the photograph? I didn't understand why this person had turned so abruptly. Why was someone out on the lake in such fog? Why had he disappeared? I got this strange feeling. Maybe in my own consciousness I made a connection. I do know that I can only connect from my own experience. I knew it was Tom Thomson. I was shocked when the film was developed. There was my phantom canoeist.

"I was drawn to paint the photograph. A good painting depicts what you have experienced. This photograph was a memory of the moment. The painting chooses you. It is always there. It never leaves. One day something triggers it. Within six months after the experience, I painted it. Then I painted over it. I wasn't ready. It didn't feel right.

"When I told people the story they agreed that it indeed could be Tom Thomson. Six or seven years later I did a small watercolour of that dramatic experience on Canoe Lake.

"Then one day, during a show in my gallery, a young man walked in. He was going to school out west. This piece of work, entitled *The Return of Tom Thomson*, was hanging in the show. The man purchased it. About a year later, he wrote to me to say that he bought the painting because

Courtesy of Jane Loftus

Few pictures exist of Winnie Trainor. Even her home in Huntsville was torn down shortly after her death. Winnie is seen here on the left.

he had seen the same man, in the same canoe, in the park. He had felt it had been a ghost himself. He was amazed to see it hanging in my gallery."

On the anniversary of Tom Thomson's death, a few people gather on the shore of Canoe Lake to see if he will appear. There is no question, for those who have seen him, that it is Tom.

As for Winnie Trainor, she never married, and she lived in Huntsville until her death. Jane Loftus pointed out that Miss Trainor would often travel to Canoe Lake and place flowers on the grave of Tom Thomson. Perhaps she never married because she knew he was still there with her. If she saw him and communicated with him, she kept it to herself.

Playwright Stina Nyquist, in her Tom Thomson play, *The Shantyman's Daughter*, had Miss Trainor say this about herself: "I'm a slob. I've been one since that summer a long time ago. I let my hair go. I have soup stains on my blouse, my stockings are rumpled, and so on and so forth. It's not that I'm a slob at heart. I'm not a natural-born slob. I just got that way, bit by bit, since that summer. But once every year, on this day, I dress up. I go to the beauty parlour, I put on this outfit, and this hat — if it's not too windy. I got this dress for a special occasion that didn't happen ..."

Gaye Clemson, born and raised in Toronto, now resides in Monterey Bay, California. In the early 1950s her father decided to make Algonquin Park a part of his life and purchased a lease on Canoe Lake. In 1954, her father and mother built a cabin on the leased land.

In the May 2006 issue of *The Muskoka Magazine*, journalist Meaghan Deemeester wrote an article entitled "Canoe Lake, Highlighting Clemson and the Thomson Mystery."

"Thomson, who was an avid and accomplished canoeist, died on the lake in July, 1917. His body was found several days after his upturned canoe was spotted floating on the lake, and despite a four-inch cut/bruise on his left temple, and fishing line tied around his ankle, the authorities quickly deemed his death an accidental drowning.

"However, the residents of Canoe Lake feel differently, believing in most cases that foul play was involved. In fact, in the late 1970s, Clemson's brother found the remains of a paddle stuck in the mud. She says, 'After washing and careful examination of its weather-worn condition and the fact that there was a "cut" out of the blade that looked like it was an exact match to an adult male's temple, he ascertained that it was in fact Tom's long-lost paddle and by inference the long-lost murder weapon. It hangs to this day, from our cabin ceiling."

Her passion for local history, and the tragic death surrounding Tom Thomson, led Clemson to create the Tom Thomson Murder Mystery Game. According to Deemeester, Clemson, in her game, looked at some of the theories behind Thomson's death:

1. Winnie Trainor is pregnant, Thomson doesn't want to marry her; she decides to do him in and make it look like an accident or he commits suicide as a way of getting out of marrying her.
2. Shannon Fraser owed him money and Thomson wanted it back in order to get a new suit to marry Trainor. He and Shannon get into an argument, Thomson falls, hits his head on the fireplace grate and dies. Fraser and Annie try to cover it up and make it look like an accident.
3. Thomson and Martin Bletcher have a disagreement about the course of the First World War at a local party and angry words are exchanged. Martin, by chance, meets Thomson the next day on the Drummer Lake Portage. They have words again, and Martin hits him with a paddle and he dies.

Deemeester also added, "According to current Ontario Parks government policy, all residential leaseholders will be obligated to either tear down or burn their buildings and ensure that the land is returned to its original state by 2017 — ironically, 100 years after the death of Thomson."

There are many unexplained events on Canoe Lake. One young girl, Sarah, found a painting tucked in a crack in a tree and an old piece of wood inscribed with a biblical quote. Does she have a Tom Thomson original? Who is creating mystical art in Algonquin Park?

There are power boats on the lake now. There are mysteries, and there are many unanswered questions for the curious visitors.

Timmins

"The City with a heart of gold" — Timmins, "The Gold Capital," located in the heartland of the greatest mineral-producing area in the Western Hemisphere.

Timmins has seen economic activity since the early French fur trade in 1678. The discovery of silver in Cobalt, in 1903, enabled Noah and Henry Timmins, general store operators, to make a small fortune. From there Noah and Henry went on to finance the development of claims that had been staked by prospectors Benny Hollinger and Alec Gillies, at Porcupine Camp, now Timmins. It was renamed in 1909 in honour of these two industrious men.

The first mining claim in the district was staked in May 1905 on the southwest shore of Nighthawk Lake by Edward Orr Taylor. The following year Reuben D'Aigle headed up a prospecting party in Tisdale Township.

The D'Aigle party made a very significant oversight. To their misfortune, they missed some fairly obvious rich gold showings that were merely covered by moss. It was Jack Wilson Massey who uncovered the Golden Staircase, as it was called, and it eventually became known as the Dome Mine.

Two Finnish prospectors, Victor Mansen and Harry Benella, made a gold discovery on Gold Island, in Nighthawk Lake, in 1907. The immediate finds, however, were not encouraging and the project was suspended. It was Charlie Auer who later staked a nearby claim that became the Nighthawk Peninsula Mine and, between 1924 and 1944, produced about $500,000 in gold.

Barber Benny Hollinger and his partner, Alec Gillies, made the first substantial strike, south of present-day Gillies Lake, in Timmins. Noah and Henry Timmins invested their money in the Hollinger interests, and the Hollinger Mine was incorporated in 1910. A property that was staked by Sandy McIntyre and Hans Buttner became the McIntyre Mine. It was later discovered that copper was also present in the mine and, by 1963, the copper ore recovered exceeded that of gold.

It was still the shanty town of Porcupine Camp in 1911, but it was beginning to grow with the help of prospectors and other investors. In July of that year disaster struck. Gale-force winds fanned a number of scattered bush fires into a massive firestorm that flattened the entire settlement and killed 200 people. Many were buried on the shore of Porcupine Lake, a location appropriately called Dead Man's Point.

The Municipality of Timmins came into being on January 1, 1912, and grew quickly. So many people came here from different parts of the world that it can be said that Timmins was "multicultural" before the rest of Canada.

The Timmins area has been a steady producer in gold production alone, more than $1.5 billion has been mined here. Immense copper, silver, and zinc reserves have been unearthed in the Kidd Creek area. This most notable discovery was announced in 1964, by the Texas Gulf Sulphur Company. Their Kidd Mine operation is now operated by Falconbridge Limited, and remains a viable metallurgical industry.

Stone is an impressive material, and the Timmins-Porcupine Chamber of Commerce understood this when they raised a 15-ton ore specimen from the Kidd Creek Mine, containing zinc, copper, silver, lead, and cadmium.

The Timmins Underground Gold Mine Tour is a great tourist attraction and is located at the Hollinger gold mine on James Reid Road. The underground portion of the tour lasts approximately 1.5 hours and is guided by retired miners who operate all of the various equipment. On the surface, visitors can pan for gold (keep all you find), view the pouring of a "Gold" brick at the Refinery, or tour the Hollinger House.

Timmins is the largest mining municipality in the world today and it is also very picturesque, with more than 500 lakes and hundreds of miles of streams. There is camping at Kettle Lake Provincial Park, 20 minutes from downtown, and it is one of Ontario's finest parks.

It is an unfortunate state of affairs, in a land of such natural beauty, to learn about the mineral rights in the area. You may think you own your property in Timmins, but you do not own the rights to what exists beneath the soil. You have "surface rights." The rest of the rights are already owned by previously staked mines. Therefore, if a copper, gold, or silver vein is discovered on your land, you could find heavy equipment digging up your backyard tomorrow.

Residents of Timmins are well aware of this unfortunate situation. Just a few years ago, a mining company decided to claim the gold tailings discovered in a city park. The trees were ripped out of the ground and the earth was removed. In a very short time there was nothing left of the park. What will it take for mankind to end the rape and pillage of the earth? To put something back where something has been taken? Perhaps the city fathers should remember their title: "City with a Heart of Gold!"

Toronto

A French fortified post named Fort Rouille was built in 1749 on the present site of the Canadian National Exhibition. Prior to this, Native fur traders travelled down the Humber River, across Lake Ontario to Fort Oswego to trade with the English on the south side of Lake Ontario.

Natives named the fort Toronto, meaning "Place of Meeting." That fort was burned by the French when it became evident that the British might take it over. An obelisk erected on the actual site, and a concrete outline in the grass of Fort Rouille, just west of the bandshell on the CNE grounds, is all that is left to tell the tale.

The British were anxious to own this new territory and negotiated with the Natives in 1787 for the land that the city of Toronto now occupies. Natives still contend that ownership of the Toronto Islands was never negotiated in the treaty, named "Toronto Purchase." This treaty encompassed an area stretching 23 kilometres (14 miles) along Lake Ontario and running northward for 48 kilometres (30 miles). In return for this, the British paid the Natives 1,700 pounds sterling and 149 barrels of goods (axes, cloth, and blankets). One year later, the southern section of land was surveyed for a townsite.

It wasn't actually settled until 1793, when John Graves Simcoe established Fort York. Simcoe called the new settlement York, in honour of the son of George III of England.

At noon, on August 27, 1793, Simcoe ordered the first royal salute to be fired to celebrate the birth of the capital of Upper Canada. To pay homage to such status, Upper Canada's first "government house" was a canvas tent.

Three years later the first parliament buildings were constructed at Front and Berkeley Streets. Unfortunately, the buildings were burned to the ground by American forces during the War of 1812. Little York defended itself bravely during the war against the American force of 2,400 soldiers. However, the Americans won the day after an eight hour battle. Not satisfied with winning, American soldiers torched York's public building and temporarily occupied the town until the British regained control.

Government officials erected a new brick government building on the same site, in 1818, and it was destroyed by fire as well. A third parliamentary building constructed west of present-day Union Station on Front Street served as the seat of the government until 1893. New buildings were then erected in Queen's Park at the head of University Avenue on April 4 of that year, and the Ontario Legislature opened its 26th session. Premier Oliver Mowat presided over the legislature.

A traveller visiting the settlement in 1798 remarked, "A dreary dismal place, not even possessing the characteristics of a village. There is no church, schoolhouse nor, in fact, any of the ordinary signs of civilization. There is no inn, and those travellers who have no friends to go to, pitch a tent and live there while they remain."

Upper Canada's capital, situated on low-lying ground, became known as Muddy York, especially in the spring. It was Bishop Strachan, an educator and the first Anglican Bishop of York, who was instrumental in the development of the settlement. Bishop Strachan founded King's College, chartered in 1827, as the first institution of higher learning in Upper Canada. King's College later became known as the University of Toronto.

The name York ceased to exist in 1834, when the settlement reverted back to the Native name, Toronto, and it was incorporated that same year as the City of Toronto, population 9,000. This grand city inhabited one square mile and extended north to Dundas Street, west to Bathurst Street, and east to Parliament Street. The first mayor of the city was William Lyon Mackenzie, a Scotsman, editor of a newspaper, and opponent of the Family Compact — the ruling class. Mackenzie's career as a reformer climaxed during the armed Rebellion of 1837. This battle was fought near Montgomery's Tavern on Yonge Street, and it ended with Mackenzie's defeat and exile.

Courtesy of Metropolitan Toronto Reference Library

Trinity College, Toronto, circa 1860.

The most famous and the longest street in Canada, Yonge Street, began as a soldier's trail in 1795. This pathway provided a route and connection to Lake Simcoe to the north. York's first industry, a tannery, opened on Yonge Street in 1812. In 1849 Yonge Street saw the city's first public transportation: four six-passenger, horse-drawn omnibuses operating between the St. Lawrence Market and the Red Lion Hotel in Yorkville. The first horse-drawn street railway in Canada appeared on Yonge Street in 1861. Electric trolleys began in 1892 on Church Street and reached a speed of 10 miles per hour. Timothy Eaton opened his first business in 1869 — a dry goods store on Yonge Street, and Robert Simpson followed suit three years later.

The first steam engine to be built in Canada was at Good's Foundry. On April 16, 1853, this quaint locomotive, named *Toronto*, was transported down Yonge Street to the permanent tracks on Front Street, at the foot of Bay Street. A month later that same locomotive headed the first train to run in Ontario. It went from Toronto to Machell's Corner, which is now

Aurora. The first train to visit Toronto on the newly completed Grand Trunk line arrived on October 27, 1856. The city's first Union Station, a small brick building at the foot of York Street, was built for joint use of the Grand Trunk, the Northern, and the Great Western Railways until a new station was opened west of York in 1873. The Union Station that we see today was started in 1914 and completed 13 years later, at which time it was opened by the Prince of Wales (later King Edward VIII) during his 1927 trip to celebrate Canada's 60th birthday.

Crime always accompanies major cities, and although we read about it every day, it certainly isn't new. By 1862 at least 12 people had been hanged in Canada, and Toronto had some stories to share. Flogging and branding were common punishments for petty larceny and other misdemeanours in the early 19th century. The hangman usually administered the lash and most often did so in public. It was also his duty to brand criminals. This was usually done on the hands or on the tongue, until 1802, when it was abolished for all but manslaughter.

York's first public execution occurred in 1798. The crime was forging an order for three shillings and sixpence. The accused was John Sullivan, a tailor. It had actually been Mike Flannery who did the forgery job. Flannery had simply used Sullivan, but upon hearing news of the discovery of the forged document, Flannery fled to the United States. Sullivan was merely the man who signed the document in order to cash it. He was sentenced to death, and confined in an old log jail situated near the present King Edward Hotel. On the day of the execution, October 11, people celebrated as if it were a public holiday. A huge crowd of men, women, and children congregated by the gallows, and there stood Sullivan waiting to be hanged. The crowd watched with bated breath. Snap went the rope. Sullivan's neck did not. The rope had broken. Not only was he the first to be hanged. He was the first to be hanged twice!

In 1816 a murder occurred on Yonge Street. Elijah Dexter shot James Vanderburg during a quarrel. Some people thought Dexter had shot in self-defence, but government officials thought otherwise. He was charged and found guilty of murder and sentenced to death. Once again the crowds gathered. People took time off from business and farm chores to watch the hanging. This time it was Reverend John Strachan who escorted Dexter to the scaffold. When Dexter appeared, the crowd cheered. Dexter had no intention of dying. He wasn't ready. At the base of the scaffold he refused to ascend. The jailer was a resourceful man. Off he went to get a horse and cart, and then placed Dexter in the vehicle with his back to the scaffold. Next he moved Dexter under the scaffold and then adjusted the noose accordingly; finally, he lashed the horse and off it bolted, leaving Dexter to hang in the air.

A gruesome murder occurred in 1819, near Whitby. It was so brutal that some citizens took the law into their own hands. The murderer never stood trial. The murderer was a Frenchman named De Benyon. Apparently, De Benyon had difficulty tolerating his 13-year-old stepson. He turned the young man out of the house on a bitter winter night. Sometime later he allowed the lad back in and proceeded to tie him up in front of the fireplace. The boy literally roasted to death while De Benyon watched. Caught in the act, he tried to escape, but his neighbours overtook him near a bridge over the Don River. No one cared to wait for the authorities. They hung him on the spot.

In 1828 two men were scheduled to hang at the same time, at York's second jail, near the northeast corner of King and Toronto Streets. It was incredible, this fascination with death. Ten thousand "concerned" citizens turned out to witness this. How far will people go to watch a hanging? Quite the distance, it would seem, since York itself had only a population of 2,000.

Women were also hung for murder. On December 14, 1837, Julia Murdock was hanged for murdering her mistress with arsenic. This hanging attracted 4,000 people.

The last recorded duel fought in York occurred on July 12, 1817, between John Ridout and Samuel Peters Jarvis. John and Samuel were good friends and had grown up as neighbours. They had fought together in the War of 1812. So why did they duel?

It wasn't the first time. John's father had thwarted them before, but this time Ridout, age 18, and Samuel, age 25, left their homes unnoticed, in the wee hours of the morning, and met in a meadow just east of the parliament buildings. The duel was set; both men paced off and fired. John Ridout was killed instantly. Although Jarvis was charged and tried for murder, he was acquitted. It would seem this was a customary practice.

Archives of Ontario

Sunnyside, Toronto, circa 1900. As busy then as it is today.

In 1852 a group of businessmen gathered together every morning to talk about and trade their stocks and bonds. Little did they know what they were starting. Today, Bay Street is the financial heart of Canada's business capital. In a conservative but impeccable building, home to the Toronto Stock Exchange since 1983, business men and woman still gather daily for the same purpose.

The Canadian National Exhibition has a long history as a place for new ideas. In its original incarnation, it had no permanent home and would move from year to year to different cities and towns in the province. It was, in fact, called the Provincial Agricultural Association Fair.

In 1879 the Provincial Legislature incorporated the "Industrial Exhibition Association of Toronto"; these were the days when grand expositions set the imagination alight. Often this was the opportunity to inform the world of marvelous new inventions — and there was no radio, television, or movie theatre to interfere with attendance or attention. One hundred thousand people came to the Exhibition that fall, on the site of the present Exhibition Place. It lasted for three weeks and the admission was 25 cents.

The Toronto Industrial Exhibition was the first in the world to use electricity and one of the first to introduce electric trains. Thomas Edison conducted many of his early experiments here, to the delight of the board of directors. He even recorded a famous message at the CNE, from Lord Stanley (who also donated the Stanley Cup), to the U.S. President. Edison was also responsible for inventing overhead power lines, the trolley pole, and electric railways — all at the Toronto Industrial Exhibition.

The most enduring symbol of the CNE is the Princes' Gates, often mistakenly called "The Princess Gates," at the entrance to the grounds. In 1927, during the visit to open Union Station, Prince Edward and his brother Prince George (later King George VI) officially opened the fair. The gates were named in their honour and the statue that sits atop them, *The Winged Victory*, has become a recognizable emblem of the CNE. The residents of the original Fort Rouille would not recognize Exhibition Place today.

There is still history in the making, in Toronto, including the end of Maple Leaf Gardens, the new Roy Thompson Hall, the Rogers Centre, the CN Tower, the spectacular Eaton Centre, Ontario Place, and many places and events. The Natives were quite right to name this place Toronto. It is a cosmopolitan centre — a great meeting place.

Trenton

Once the Hollywood of Canada, Trenton was not so glamorous back in 1790, when the first settlers arrived. James Smith, a country judge from New York, and John Richard Bleecker from Albany were the first to settle at the mouth of the River Trent.

Smith built a log cabin on the east bank of the river and just a few months later John Bleecker put one on the west bank. Bleecker died in 1807 and his widow, Mary, operated an inn and a ferry service on the site for many years. Mary sold the property to Henry Ripsom, a Loyalist who erected the first gristmill on the Trent 3.2 kilometres (2 miles) upriver from the mouth.

Trenton's early settlers were predominantly United Empire Loyalists who arrived there in the 1790s. Adam Henry Meyers, however, a native of Germany, was the first to open a general store in this settlement, which was initially named Trent Port.

In 1829 John Strachan, the first Anglican Bishop of York (Toronto) established lots on his property in the Trenton area to create a community named Annwood. Strachan was a visionary. He encouraged craftsmen to settle on his land and donated a site for St. George's Anglican Church. The church, Trenton's oldest, was constructed in 1845, replacing an earlier frame structure. Despite his efforts, Annwood eventually merged with Trenton.

Another influential figure was Captain Sheldon Hawley, who along with his brother-in-law Josiah, assisted in the further development of the community. They established a lumber business and a mercantile store. Trenton quickly became an important lumbering centre. From here the lumber was shipped to Montreal and Quebec City. Two large steam-powered mills, owned by Gilmour and J. Flindall, set up operations on the east side of the Trent. On an island in the Bay of Quinte, there were the mills of Baker and Company and C. Weaver Esq. At the time the Rathun Lumber Company of Trenton was the largest operation in all of Ontario, harvesting timber in North Hastings.

By the 1860s the lumber industry in Trenton was shipping 5,000,000 cubic feet of square white pine by raft annually to the Quebec market. Several hundred thousand logs (each season) were also shipped to American ports.

By the mid-1870s, the Gilmour Company employed at least 400 men in their planing mill, the box plant, and in the sash, door, and veneer factory. Sawdust from this sawmill was used to provide fill for many of Trenton's building sites.

In the 1830s construction started on the Trent Canal. Trent Port became the gateway to a water system which eventually linked Bay of Quinte and Georgian Bay.

Trent Port had a population of 1,500 residents when it was incorporated as a village and officially named Trenton in 1853. Three years later the Grand Trunk Railway steamed into the village. Trenton became the hub of transportation with a network of three railways for a brief interlude.

Trenton became one of Ontario's major industrial towns when Robert Waddell established the Trenton Bridge and Engine Works in the 1870s. The company manufactured steel and iron bridges, iron piers, engine boilers, tugs, and steamboats.

On Dominion Day, 1880, Trentonians held a gala celebration in honour of their new status as a town. Dr. W.H. Day was elected as Trenton's first mayor.

Trenton suffered its first serious setback in 1910 when the Gilmour Sash and Door Factory burned to the ground. It made a strong comeback when it was chosen as the site for the British Chemical Company's multi-million-dollar ammunitions plant during the First World War. Tragedy struck again on Thanksgiving Day 1918, when a fire broke out in that factory and ignited explosives that blew the buildings apart. Amazingly enough, no one was killed.

Archives of Ontario

Trenton circa 1931. The film industry here was once thought to be Ontario's Hollywood.

The fireworks continued throughout the night and the town telephone operator, Eva Curtis, stayed at her switchboard to keep vital communications open. For courage in a danger zone, she and seven others were awarded the medal of the Order of the British Empire.

Welcome to Hollywood! That's how it seemed in 1919 when Trenton was chosen by the government as the site for a film plant. Numerous films, including *The Great Shadow* and *Carry on Sergeant*, were produced here. The only reminder of these bygone days is a street in Trenton named Film Street.

During the Depression, Trenton and its residents managed to escape some financial hardships thanks to Senator William Alexander Fraser. Through his efforts Trenton was chosen to be the home of the Royal Canadian Air Force. The town's unemployed were quickly hired to build the airport and base. In the Second World War, this military centre served as the Commonwealth Air Training Base. In 1949 Memorial Gates at the airport entrance were erected to commemorate the contribution made by the base during the war. Over the years the military presence has contributed greatly to the economy and social stability of the town.

In the 1950s Trenton's industrial base included 25 major manufacturing companies, including Quaker Oats, Delft Gelatin, and S.H. Camp & Company, a subsidiary of one of the world's largest manufacturers of surgical garments and braces.

The downtown core was devastated by three fires in 1978. Merchants and town officials rallied to the task of rebuilding, and by midsummer of the same year a 26-store shopping complex replaced what the fire had destroyed.

On July 1, 1980, exactly 100 years after Trenton was incorporated as a town, it became a city. Now, Trenton may be best known as a tourist centre. It has many claims to fame, but for me it was my start in life because my mother called it home.

I, personally, have fond memories of summers with my family (the Gauens).

Whitby

Whitby certainly has a great history of characters, including at least one very mysterious murderer.

The early settlement of the district began around Whitby's natural harbor at the lakeshore and along the Kingston Road. Jabez Lynde settled here on the Kingston Road at Lynde's Creek in 1804. Samuel Cochrane soon arrived and a Mr. Storey and a Mr. Losie opened shops in the area circa 1818.

The first post office between Toronto and Port Hope was opened by J.B. Warren in 1823. In 1835 John Hamer opened a store, and the settlement became known as Hamer's Corners at what is now Dundas and Anderson Streets.

The harbor was called Windsor Bay and it was a thriving grain port, with a storehouse, a tramway, and a warehouse, in the 1830s.

By October 1836 Peter Perry, the MPP for Lennox and Addington Counties near the Bay of Quinte, lost his seat in Parliament and moved to the area. He purchased most of the land around the present four corners of the town. This wealthy entrepreneur and visionary built a store on the site of the present-day Bank of Commerce as well as a large brick home. He hired a provincial land surveyor to draw up a town plan for the area around the four corners in 1844. Perry then encouraged merchants and businessmen to settle in his community; this area became the centre of commerce instead of Hamer's Corners. The four corners of this settlement were soon named Perry's Corners.

By 1848 the harbor had become so busy that a plank road was constructed to Port Perry to facilitate the movement of grain and lumber

Courtesy of Whitby Historical Society

Whitby circa 1880s. Looking closely at the picture, Whitby might have resembled Dodge City in the American southwest.

from the northern part of the region. Conflict arose over the name of the harbour, since "Windsor," a name favoured by many residents, already existed elsewhere in the province. The name Whitby, from a seaside town in Yorkshire, England, was then assigned to the area. At least they got to keep the initial. Whitby was incorporated as a town in 1855.

Sheriff Nelson Reynolds may not have been a Wyatt Earp, but he was an adventuresome fellow. A God-fearing man, he always mixed a taste for personal glory with his somewhat righteous goals. Few citizens of Whitby knew that in his youth he had been treasonous, part of the failed Rebellion of Upper Canada against the Family Compact. He was the man who would one day build the castle of his dreams, right in Whitby.

Born in Kingston in 1814, Reynolds rose to lead his own cavalry regiment there during the Rebellion of 1837. Government officials kept a watchful eye on him, since he never hid his criticism of the Family

Compact. They were suspicious of Reynolds; they worried that instead of leading his troops in defence of Kingston against attack, he might join the opposing forces.

On the eve of February, 1837, an alarm was sounded, warning of the invasion by rebel forces. Thinking this could be the night that Reynolds would turn, patriotic officials ordered government troops to surround Reynolds and his men and to charge Reynolds with high treason. It had been a false alarm, and before Reynolds could lead a charge, he and his men were captured. Of course he refused arrest and stood his ground, until a musket cracked and a lead ball found its mark in his leg. Fearing for his life, he broke free and escaped across the American border with the help of his men.

In July 1838 he returned and surrendered to government officials. Led under guard to Fort Henry, he was imprisoned and charged with high treason. He conducted his own defence and set out to prove his innocence. He managed to do this because of the lack of evidence necessary to convict him.

With the news of his release, the soldiers of his former regiment rushed to meet their old friend. To rejoice in his freedom, they picked him up and carried him through the streets of Kingston.

Fourteen years later, in 1854, he was appointed sheriff of Ontario County. His duties included land arrangements, the signing of legal documents, and the foreclosure of mortgages.

It wasn't until 1859 that the sheriff began construction of Tralfager Castle at the east end of Dunlop Street in Whitby. This was his dream house, and because he hoped to gain the attention of royalty, should they visit, he spared no cost in its construction.

When it was finished, his elegant castle was built of stone, a monument to fine craftsmanship. Visitors could imagine they were in the English countryside when they gazed upon this dwelling.

His dream came true when, in 1864, Prince Arthur, third son of Queen Victoria and later the governor-general of Canada, visited the sheriff's castle. And, of course, Sir John A. MacDonald, fond of a dining invitation, also visited en route.

In 1872 the purse strings drew to a close. Sadly, elegance and extravagance cost Reynolds his castle. Although forced to sell his dream,

Sheriff Reynolds never lost sight of his vision. The moment Trafalger sold, Reynolds built again. This time his castle was a miniature replica of the former. At the age of 67, the sheriff slept his last night. In the meantime Trafalger Castle was taken over and converted to the Ontario Ladies College.

A mysterious murder occurred years later in Whitby. It happened in the early hours of December 11, 1914. Twenty-one-year-old telegraph operator William Stone Jr. would sit quietly at his desk in the Whitby Train Station recording the trains that passed and noting any telegraph messages. This night seemed like any other. Nothing really exciting ever happened as the townspeople slept in their beds. Something was brewing that night, however, and it was about to explode. At 12:37 a.m., a shot was fired from the darkness. Billy Stone toppled out of his chair and landed with a thud on the floor. By some miracle he managed to crawl to a phone and call for help. Leslie Cormack, the operator for the local Bell Telephone switchboard, answered his call.

"Get the chief, quick; I've been shot," gasped Stone.

"Who did it?" responded Cormack, while she dialed Police Chief Charles F. MacGrotty.

Stone answered, "I don't know, but get the chief quick".

As Chief MacGrotty picked up the phone, there was silence.

Was William dead?

The chief rushed out and headed downtown to fetch the night watchman, John Patterson. Together they travelled to the train station. It was an eerie sight. The shade on William's desk light had been turned to cast its rays of lights on the tracks. Peering in the window they saw Stone lying on the office floor. The telephone receiver was under his lifeless body.

The chief forced the door open and quickly rushed to Stone. He was dead. The chief peered around the room but saw no indication of a struggle. Was robbery a motive? He checked the cash drawer but nothing had been taken. He turned to William's entry book. The last recorded train was a freight train going east at 12:15 a.m., approximately 20 minutes prior to the alarming phone call. Who killed Stone?

The chief then discovered the bloody imprint of a hand on one of the cabinets. Stone's hands were clean of blood. Could this be the handprint of the killer?

News of the murder spread and speculation abounded — a passing tramp, perhaps. The call went out to Ontario Provincial Police Inspector William Greer.

Two leads led to dead ends. The mystery seemed to deepen when Stone's sister reported having had a dream the week before her brother's death in which she had seen him shot at work in the same manner as the actual crime.

An inquest into the murder began in January 1915, and continued intermittently until June when another event shed some light on the crime. Apparently, William Stone Sr., the murder victim's father, had arrived home late on the evening of June 18 after consuming some spirits in a nearby hotel. He thought he had become a suspect.

Stone Sr. went to pieces when he was called as a witness at the inquest. Somehow he had assumed that he was now the target of the investigation. He was sure that the authorities were linking him to his son's murder. Unable to bear up, Billy's Father set out that night to end his life. At the Grand Trunk Railway, not too far from the scene of the crime, he lay down on the tracks and waited. William Stone Sr. was killed instantly. Was he the murderer?

It was plausible. William Stone Sr. did have a reputation as a heavy drinker and had appeared in court relatively recently on charges of assaulting his daughter while under the influence. He had even threatened to kill her. Had he killed his own son for insurance money?

Harry Birmingham, a close friend of William Stone Jr., had been the last person to see him before his death. Birmingham claimed he had left the station at 11:30 p.m. on the night of the murder. Birmingham had apparently said that he and Stone had been fired at in a field by Corbett's Crossing (Thickson and the CNR). However, Birmingham denied this story at the inquest.

Two bus drivers who had often chatted with the victim when they arrived at the station to pick up passengers testified that one, and sometimes two, revolvers were kept in the drawer of Stone's desk. Were the revolvers in the desk drawer on the night of the murder? The police found no revolvers in the drawer. Birmingham owned an old revolver, but the .38 calibre bullet that killed Stone did not fit his gun. Birmingham was cleared.

Brian Winters, Whitby's historical archivist, first reported this story in the local paper and adds, "One Whitby resident recalls that many years later, in the 1920s or 30s a man was executed in the United States. As the trap door dropped, he confessed to a murder in Whitby. But it was too late to find out what murder it was, for he was dead before he could complete what he was saying."

The murder of Billy Stone remains unsolved. Who really left their bloody handprint at the scene of the crime? Does Billy still haunt the old Train Station?

A famous sheriff and a famous murder — just a glimpse of the colourful history of this portside town.

Bibliography

Abbott, George F. *Abbott's Guide to Ottawa, Hull & Vicinity*, 2nd Edition. Publisher unknown: Ottawa, 1911.

Barlow, Shirley. *Gravenhurst: An Album of Memories and Mysteries*. Gravenhurst: Gravenhurst Book Committee, 1993.

Beattie, Owen and John Geiger. *Frozen in Time*. Saskatoon: Western Producer Prairie Books: 1987.

Boyer, Robert. *Woodchester Villa*. Bracebridge: Bracebridge Historical Society, 1982.

Boyle, Terry. *Under This Roof*. Toronto: Doubleday, 1980.

Boyle, Terry. *Ontario Memories*. Toronto: Polar Bear Press, 1998.

Craig, W. Arnot. *Little Tales of Old Port Hope*. Port Hope: Guide Publishing, 1966.

Conway, Abbott. *A History of Beardmore and Company Limited*. Toronto: Canada Packers Inc., 1990.

Farmer, Samuel. *On the Shores of Scugog*. Port Perry: *Port Perry Star*, 1934.

Fletcher, Katharine. *Capital Walks*. Toronto: McClelland & Stewart, 1993.

Fraser, Mary. *Joseph Brant, Thayendanegea*. Burlington: Joseph Brant Museum, 1969.

Guillet, Edwin C. *Toronto: From Trading Post to Great City*. Toronto: Ontario Publishing Company, 1939.

Hunt, Maureen. *A Thumb Nail Sketch of Early Huntsville*. Toronto: Boston Mills Press, 1998.

Johnson, Leo A. *History of the County of Ontario*, 1615–1875. Whitby: Corporation of the County of Ontario, 1973.

Killan, Gerald. *David Boyle*. Toronto: University of Toronto Press, 1983.

Malcolmson, Patricia. *To Preserve and Defend*. Kingston: McGill-Queen's University Press, 1976.

Mika, Nick and Helma. *Places in Ontario*. Belleville: Mika Publishing, 1977.

Mika, Nick and Helma. *Belleville, the Seat of Hastings County*. Belleville: Mika Publishing, 1986.

Murray, Florence. B. *Muskoka and Haliburton 1615–1875*. Toronto: University of Toronto Press, 1963.

Paudash, Johnston. *Coming of the Mississaga*. Ontario Historical Society Papers and Records V.1, 1905.

Philpot, Andre L. *A Species of Adventure*. Marmora: Irontown Publications, 1990.

Reynolds, Nila. *Bancroft, A Bonanza of Memories*. Bancroft: Bancroft Centennial Committee, 1979.

Stafford, David. *Camp X*. Toronto: Lester & Orpen Dennys, 1986.

Toronto Civic Historical Committee. *Historic Toronto*. 1953.

Wing, Agnes I. *History of Parry Sound*. Privately published: date unknown.

Newspapers

"Gravenhurst Was Ablaze 100 Years," *Muskoka Advance*, September 20, 1987.

"The Great Fire," *Huntsville Forester*, April 13, 1894.

"The Most Mysterious Wreck" *Imperial Oil Fleet News* (1965), Vol 17, No. 2: 3–5.

Pryke, Susan, "From Hospital to Prison Camp to Fine Hotel." *The Muskokan*, July 30, 1992.

"Steamships Used in Huntsville's Early Years," *Huntsville Hearld-News Centennial Supplement*, March 19, 1986.

"Who Shot Billy Stone?" *Whitby Free Press*, December 8, 1984.

Index

Of Related Interest

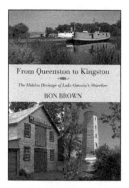

From Queenston to Kingston
by Ron Brown
9781554887163
$26.99 £15.99

Whether you hike, bike, ride the rails, or drive, the shore of Lake Ontario can yield a treasure trove of heritage sites and natural beauty — if you know where to look.

Travel with Ron Brown as he probes the shoreline of the Canadian side of Lake Ontario to discover its hidden heritage. Explore "ghost ports," forgotten coves, historical lighthouses, rum-running lore, and even the location of a top-secret spy camp. The area also contains some unusual natural features, including a mysterious mountain-top lake, sand dunes, and the rare albars of Prince Edward County.

From small communities to the megacity of Toronto, history lives on in the buildings, bridges, canals, rail lines, and homes that have survived, and in the stories, both well-known and long-forgotten, of the people and places no longer here. In *From Queenston to Kingston*, Ron Brown provides today's explorer's with a window into Ontario's not so distant past and shares a hope that, in future, progress and historical preservation go hand in hand.

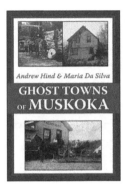

Ghost Towns of Muskoka
by Andrew Hind and Maria Da Silva
9781550027969
$24.99 £12.99

Ghost Towns of Muskoka explores the tragic history of a collection of communities from across Muskoka whose stars have long since faded. Today, these ghost towns are merely a shadow — or spectre — of what they once were. Some have disappeared entirely, having been swallowed by regenerating forests, while others have been reduced to foundations, forlorn buildings, and silent ruins. A few support a handful of inhabitants, but even these towns are wrapped in a ghostly shroud.

But this book isn't only about communities that have died. Rather it is about communities that lived, vibrantly at that, if only for a brief time. It's about the people whose dreams for a better life these villages represented; the people who lived, loved, laboured, and ultimately died in these small wilderness settlements. And it's about an era in history, those early heady days of Muskoka settlement when the forests were flooded with loggers and land-hungry settlers.

Unsolved
True Canadian Cold Cases
by Robert J. Hoshowsky
9781554887392
$24.99 £14.99

Despite advances in DNA testing, forensics, and the investigative skills used by police, hundreds of crimes remain unsolved across Canada. With every passing day trails grow colder and decades can pass before a new lead or witness comes forward … if one comes forward.

In *Unsolved*, Robert J. Hoshowsky examines twelve crimes that continue to haunt us. Some cases are well-known, while others have virtually disappeared from the public eye. All of the cases remain open, and many are being re-examined by police using the latest tools and technology. Hoshowsky takes the reader through all aspects of the crimes and how police are trying to solve them using three-dimensional facial reconstructions, DNA testing, age-enhanced drawings, original crime scene photos, and more.

None of the individuals profiled in *Unsolved* deserved their fate, but their stories deserve to be told and their killers need to be brought to justice.

Available at your favourite bookseller.

DUNDURN
www.dundurn.com

What did you think of this book?
Visit www.dundurn.com for reviews, videos, updates, and more!